WARRIOR ENDORSEMENTS

"I first met Lorenzo at a Culver City Kickboxing event. As a fighter, we always remember other fighters that stand out on fight cards. At this event, only two combatants stood out: Eddie Mapula and Lorenzo Rodriguez. Both had a stage presence in the ring. They had style and grace as champions. Lorenzo was an exciting, flashy, and charismatic fighter to watch. After retiring from fighting, I worked out at the El Monte Self-Defense School for about two years. Lorenzo never charged me. I have met many fighters, trainers, and promoters during my fighting years. Among them, Lorenzo was a genuine and honest person. He never took advantage of others. I consider him a brother, a real friend. He has the Bushido spirit. He is a martial artist, in the true sense of the word. He is someone you want in your corner."

—Danny "Magic" Lopez, 3rd Degree Black Belt, Si Lum Kung Fu, IKBA California Middleweight Champion, IKBA World Middleweight and IKBA World Jr. Middleweight Champion Stuntman and 2nd Unit Director, Producer, Director, and Actor for "When Death Come Knocking" and Director of Photography and Film Editor for Emmy nominated, "Camacho Experiment," on El Rey Network.

"Lorenzo and I followed similar life paths growing up. He lived in South El Monte, and I grew up in Tijuana and San Ysidro. We both had our share of fights as youths. Likewise, we were both dedicated to our martial arts training, and had a determination to prevail in any street or tournament altercation that came our way. As a result, we became champions. I've been told that at one time Lorenzo wanted to fight me for my championship belts. Unfortunately, our paths never crossed, but I know it would have been a great fight! I have always known him to be a humble and sincere person. We remain martial art friends to this day."

—Eddie Mápula, 10th Degree Black Belt and a 3-time World Kickboxing/Karate Champion USA Martial Arts, Taekwondo, KRO1, Tijuana, Baja, and California Halls of Fame inductee. Founder and President of Black Belt Development and Life Coach Instructor

"I knew Grandmaster Lorenzo Rodriguez as "Papa." As a troubled young man needing a positive mentor in my life, he took me into his home and gave me purpose. I had no background in boxing or martial arts. Papa taught me how to train and fight in kickboxing and helped me win championships. More importantly, he gave me confidence to change my life and be a better person. Papa's life experience as a fighter and martial arts master is really a true tale about perseverance and leadership. I am proud to be a small part of that story."

—Scott Thorson, former Super Lightweight, Lightweight, and Welterweight Kickboxing Champion; Domestic Violence Crisis Response Manager and Public Speaker

"I originally studied LimaLama under Richard Nuñez in Montebello, California, in 1978 at the YWCA. I had already heard of Lorenzo, who had a phenomenal reputation among fighters, when I met him at a tournament. I was impressed by all his technical knowledge—very fluid, fast, and effective strikes. I began training at the El Monte Self Defense School. I was there nearly 10 years. Lorenzo never charged me for training but always asked me to help train others. I was a sponge, wanting to learn all I could from anyone. It was the best time in my life. Lorenzo's school had all the equipment, bags, boxing ring, and mats. Full-contact karate and kickboxing tournaments were on the rise at the time. Lorenzo introduced me to many great fighters, trainers, and promoters during this period. He sparred with me in the ring and made me a better fighter. He was in my corner for fights, giving me a tactical advantage. He was not just my trainer/manager, he became my friend. I sincerely thank Lorenzo from the bottom of my heart for his guidance and support throughout the years. Without him I would not have won championships."

—James Saldaña, 4th Degree, LimaLama. IKBA and WKA Heavyweight Champion and WKBA, North American Heavyweight Champion

"My brother Refugio and I first met Lorenzo in the early days of Full-contact and kickboxing tournaments. My brother and I were first-generation black belts under Grandmaster Ed Parker's Kenpo system. We were yin and yang to each other, which is reflected on our gi patch. Refugio was a fighter, and I was drawn to the artistic forms and techniques, competing in Katas. Refugio never fought Lorenzo, but they both had a mutual respect for each other as fighters. The three of us worked together to train and promote fighters and events. Lorenzo was a great representative for LimaLama. I believe he was the first LimaLama master to fight in kickboxing and become a champion. Refugio passed away in April of 2022, but I know he would agree with me in saying that Lorenzo is a true martial arts professional and a gentleman. He came from a period when martial arts practitioners were respectful of other combatants and fighting styles. His story is an honest and revealing look at kickboxing history; but more importantly, he remains a positive role model for today's fighters."

—**Jesús Flores, 10th Degree Dan, American Kenpo Karate. Flores Brothers Kenpo Karate Studio, Oxnard CA**

LIMALAMA

THE AUTOBIOGRAPHY OF
LORENZO "THUMPER" RODRIGUEZ

WARRIOR

The powerful story of a fighter's incredible journey from street fights and Karate tournaments to Kickboxing Champion.

WITH
RICHARD ALVARADO

LimaLama Warrior, The Autobiography of Lorenzo "Thumper" Rodriguez: The Powerful Story of A Fighter's Incredible Journey from Street Fights and Karate Tournaments to Kickboxing Champion
© 2024, Richard Alvarado. All rights reserved.
Published by Órale Press, Upland, California

ISBN 978-1-7342492-2-4 (paperback)
ISBN 978-1-7342492-3-1 (eBook)
Library of Congress Control Number: 2023920587

www.purochisme.org

Without limiting the rights under copyright reserved above, no part of this publication may be reproduced, stored in or introduced into a retrieval system, or transmitted in any form or by any means (electronic, mechanical, photocopying, recording or otherwise whether now or hereafter known), without the prior written permission of both the copyright owner and the above publisher of this book, except by a reviewer who wishes to quote brief passages in connection with a review written for insertion in a magazine, newspaper, broadcast, website, blog or other outlet in conformity with United States and International Fair Use or comparable guidelines to such copyright exceptions.

This book is intended to provide accurate information with regard to its subject matter and reflects the opinion and perspective of the author. However, in times of rapid change, ensuring all information provided is entirely accurate and up-to-date at all times is not always possible. Therefore, the author and publisher accept no responsibility for inaccuracies or omissions and specifically disclaim any liability, loss or risk, personal, professional or otherwise, which may be incurred as a consequence, directly or indirectly, of the use and/or application of any of the contents of this book.

Publication managed by AuthorImprints.com

This book is dedicated to the Rodriguez family, my LimaLama family of martial art practitioners, and other professional fighters around the world.
—*Lorenzo Rodriguez*

CONTENTS

Foreword i
Prelude v
Introduction 1

1 The Origins of LimaLama 9
    The Grandmaster 9
    Birth of a Samoan Warrior 11
    Tino's Formal Martial Arts Training 12
    Birth of LimaLama 15
    Establishing the TILOA 17

2 The Birth of a Warrior 23
    "Curtidor" 23
    East Los Angeles 26
    La Verne 30
    South El Monte 35
    Training Under Master Sal 38
    My First Tournament 42
    Chiquito Pero Picoso 45
    The Cleland House 49
    Grandmaster Tino 54
    Tournament Fights 56
    The Bull Ring 58
    "Whitey" 62

Life Is Not a Sport	64
The Bud Boys	65
Grandmaster Woo	67
Gang Bangers	71
Becoming an Army Grunt	75

3 Honing the Sword ... 81
Charlie Company Enforcer	81
Mad Dog and the Wrestler	86
Battle with Bravo Company	88
The "Ringer" of South Korea	91
Ba Gua Quan	96
Underground Fights	103
Comfort Clerk	106

4 Becoming a Champion ... 111
Back in the USA	111
The California Kid	115
Sal Esquivel's LimaLama Incorporated	119
El Monte Self Defense School	124
Ark Wong's School	128
Thumper	130
The IKBA Circuit	132
The Championship Fights	139
The Jet Center	146
My Last Championship Fight	150
Training Under Grandmaster Tino	155

5 The Next Generation ... 163
Smokers and the Mighty Mites	163
Miguel Reyes	168
Junkyard Brawl	170

Scott Thorson 177
The Pelenque 184

6 Mixed Martial Arts 187
A Different Fight Journey 187
Team Quest 189
El Pachuco 191
Joe Sarkissian 193
Cutman 198
El Padre de LimaLama, Mexico 200
The 9th Degree 204

Epilogue 209
Acknowledgments 231
Glossary Of Terms 233
References 239

FOREWORD

MARTIAL ARTS. IT IS a term that is impossible to define with just one meaning. It is commonly referred to as a collection of combat skills that can be traced back for perhaps thousands of centuries. But today, the term *martial arts* is defined by how we perceive it and how it relates to our own life experiences.

When I was a teenager, my father had instructed my brother and me to learn the art of judo at the Japanese Community Center in Sun Valley, California, for one full year. I was excited to begin, and my friend Donald and I were the youngest of the students. Back in the 1960s, they wouldn't accept any student under 16, but since we were members of the center, they allowed us to train. Although I was excited about learning judo, my first day was filled with being tossed around by the instructor like a rag doll. I don't even remember hitting the ground. I hated every class from that day on, but my father insisted we continue judo training for at least the full year.

The day after my one-year judo prison was over, I quit. However, not long after, an incident occurred, and I knew then that martial arts would be part of my life forever. It was fifth grade, and the school bully set his sights on me while playing dodgeball during recess. He jumped on my back and, without a thought, I executed a flip I learned in judo. There he went to the ground. The entire school witnessed the event and even applauded. That was the last day I was bullied from elementary school through high school. And the first day, I would happily seek martial arts training again.

Growing up the 1960s was an amazing time as Asian martial arts instructors immigrated to America and did their best to open commercial schools and begin teaching their art forms. Although judo was the most popular form of martial arts in the 1960s, karate and kung fu schools began popping up in a few places. Martial Arts tournament fever during the late 1960s and early 1970s was at an all-time high. People like Chuck Norris and Joe Lewis, who had learned martial arts while stationed overseas in the military, became our biggest tournament champions.

The 1971 release of *Billy Jack* became an American cult favorite martial arts film. The then-unknown fighting art of hapkido, introduced by Bong Soo Han, made Tom Laughlin's Billy Jack character a hero. Likewise, the Shaw Brothers Studio made martial arts movies throughout the '60s, '70s, and '80s, producing around 1,000 martial arts films, some becoming the most popular and significant Chinese-language films of the period. And who can deny the martial arts attention Bruce Lee brought to the screen. His on-screen persona changed the world of martial arts forever. Martial arts schools began popping up all over the country—Ed Parker's American Kenpo Karate, Bruce Lee's Jeet Kune Do, and Tino Tuiolosega's LimaLama, to name just a few. As they say, "It was a whole new ballgame."

The mid-1970s was a turning point in martial arts history. Until this time, tournament fighting was based on a tag-and-point system. Although there were a few broken ribs and noses, striking was minimal. The boxing world discounted martial

FOREWORD

arts, saying that it was ineffective and that none of the techniques would work in a real confrontation. That all changed when full-contact karate, later called kickboxing, was introduced. Instead of short spurts of fighting to tag an opponent and score a point, fighters would battle three-minute rounds and win by knockout, injury, or judges' scorecards. It was a new evolution for martial arts, and almost everyone was excited about the fighting arts transformation.

However, what seemed like a great idea turned into an immediate tragedy for most martial arts tournament fighters. The greatest point fighters stepped into the ring, and as quickly as they entered, they jumped back out. Tournament fighters were not used to getting hit directly in the face or even lasting the full three-minute rounds. Traditional techniques were not as effective with boxing gloves, and many movements didn't have the impact they had in the dojo. Full-contact karate was being bashed by those within who couldn't make it in the ring. Its destiny was literally on the ropes until a few individuals such as Benny Urquidez, Joe Lewis, Jeff Smith, and Bill Wallace played a major role in bringing positive attention to kickboxing.

Training for this new karate sport had to include a variety of non-martial arts training such as boxing, running, weight training, and calisthenics. Kickboxing evolved into a whole new category for the martial arts world. Women also got into the picture as Lilly Rodriguez and later Graciela Casillas opened the doors for female Kickboxers.

I mention these little slices of history because the martial arts field is always evolving. From judo movements to karate punching, kung fu animal strikes, taekwondo kicks, kickboxing and muay Thai combinations, XMA performing, and mixed martial arts (MMA) grappling; I was glad to be alive when most of it started and see the martial arts world transform before my eyes.

Ultimately, for any one of us who steps into the martial arts world, our main goal is to become a better person. The story of Lorenzo Rodriguez, his introduction to LimaLama in 1968, and his quest to be the best fighter inside and outside the ring is also the story about a young man who found confidence and internal peace from practicing and teaching martial arts. For him and other martial artists, mastering the fighting arts helps us to pursue and achieve new goals for our families, friends, and students. It is the way to uphold our honor yet remain humble and at peace.

This may explain why the term *martial arts* has a different meaning for people based on their own personal experiences. But as martial arts fighter and trainer Arnold Urquidez once said, "The martial arts made me a better person." And that, my friends, we all can agree on.

Michael Matsuda
President/Founder, Martial Arts History Museum

PRELUDE

I BEGAN TRAINING IN THE martial arts at 10 years of age, in Chinese kung fu. It took 12 years to achieve a black belt. After three years of training and competing in point fighting competitions, I realized that it was not a true test of my martial arts skills. It was more of a game of speed and tag. In fact, if you hit your opponent too hard or in the face, you got disqualified. So this is when I started to look into kickboxing and boxing. Full contact was going to be the only true test of one's abilities.

Our kung fu school, received an invitation from the El Monte Self Defense School to come and compete in a full-contact kickboxing tournament. A handful of fellow students and I went to compete. When I walked through the door, I looked around and examined the gym. It was rather large and had high ceilings like a warehouse. Everything was spaced out, and the floor was all concrete. I thought to myself, *These guys are rolling around and falling on this? We are definitely going to get the challenge we are looking for right here.* That is when I met Lorenzo Rodriguez for the first time. He approached us with a big smile on his face, his arms open, welcoming everyone and shaking everyone's hand. He told us all to make ourselves comfortable, find a spot for our things, wrap up, and stretch out; we'd be starting shortly.

On that day, every one of us got a true test of our skills. We all left with lumps and bumps and a feeling of pride because, whether we won or lost, we did it! We stood in front of someone we didn't know, and when the bell rang, fought to defend ourselves. Lorenzo held these tournaments on a regular basis every two or three months. I was definitely going to compete in these.

As time went on, the tournaments grew. No longer just a couple of schools coming to compete, but dozens would come, the crowds larger, the popularity growing. They became so popular that eventually the California State Athletic Commission came in and shut them down. They told Lorenzo that he couldn't put on a fighting competition like this without them being regulated by a governing body or there would be fines. This motivated Lorenzo to start the Western Kickboxing Federation (WKF). So now, all competitors had to be licensed by the California State Athletic Commission and have a physical by a doctor, and all fights were documented and put on file.

Creating the WKF had a positive effect. Not only were the events regulated and documented, but they were much larger and held in much classier venues—places like the Hyatt Regency Hotel in Long Beach, the Red Lion Inn in Ontario, the Disneyland Hotel, the San Bernardino Sports Arena, several different YMCAs, and youth centers around L.A. and San Bernardino. This made them more prestigious and more desirable competitions. And, with everything being regulated and documented, it supported a pathway for champions. Now there were title holders in all weight divisions, a goal for fighters to compete.

With Lorenzo Rodriguez at the helm of doing all the match-making and keeping the fights at top quality, it was very successful. Competitors were coming from all over, not just the local schools. They came from California as well as Nevada,

PRELUDE

Mexico, Arizona, and so on. He was always matching up fair fights. There were never any mismatches: the best fought the best and beginners fought beginners. As I continued to compete, I ultimately became an amateur champion. I took three titles for the WKF: The WKF California State Champ, the WKF US Welterweight Champ, and the WKF North American Champ.

Lorenzo wanted to expand the WKF. He wanted the champions to fight other champions from other organizations across the country and even other countries. I can still remember traveling to Mexico with Lorenzo to watch a kickboxing tournament and make a challenge to the Mexican champion in an attempt to unify titles. The Mexican champ had fought well that night and won. Right after the fight we stepped into the ring and made the challenge. For a split second, the whole place got quiet, and I thought to myself, *Well, we aren't getting out of here without a fight.* But the champ accepted the challenge, everyone applauded, and we left peacefully. Even though the fight never materialized, these are the types of things Lorenzo would do for his champions and to expand the notoriety of the WKF. He would always make you feel welcome and be happy to see you. This made me feel proud and honored to be a champion for him and the WKF.

As I continued to move forward in my career, I started to compete in other states and for other organizations, and I took my fourth amateur welterweight world title for an organization based out of the Midwest called the United Kickboxing Federation (UKF). I continued to compete and successfully defend all of my amateur titles. As a pro, I continued to be successful and ultimately took five titles as a pro, four of them for the International Kickboxing Karate Council (IKKC). I became an IKKC US Muay Thai Champ, IKKC North American Champ, IKKC Intercontinental Muay Thai champ and IKKC

Middleweight World Champion. The fifth title I took as a pro was for the World Boxing Council (WBC) as a National Muay Thai Champion.

I owe a great deal of my fighting success to Lorenzo. Not only did he help throughout my entire amateur career, but he made me broaden my understanding of the martial arts by showing me different techniques. He showed me that there was more than one way to throw a punch, kick, or block and slip. He was always helpful and willing to help a fighter improve. He never tried to steal a fighter from another trainer or school or even another promoter. He always wanted the best for you and wanted to develop great fighters and put on the best kickboxing show possible.

He was never negative or degrading, only positive and supportive. I can honestly say that my success in the sport of kickboxing started at the El Monte Self Defense School. That is where I stepped into the kickboxing ring for the first time. Lorenzo's students were always formidable and tough fighters in the ring. You never took them for granted. His students came ready to fight. I am grateful to have gained knowledge from him. I am proud to have known him as a trainer and promoter. More importantly, I'm grateful and honored to be a friend of such a dignified and honorable man. He truly helped me in my life, not only with success in kickboxing, but also in the successful kickboxing and boxing gym I own and operate today in Victorville, California.

So, to my good friend Lorenzo Rodriguez, I say thank you very much for everything you have done for me in my career and in my life to help me become the champion and man I am today.

Sifu Craig "The Bullet" Buchanan
Owner/Proprietor, The BulletHole Training Center,
Victorville, CA

INTRODUCTION

THE CREATION OF THIS book began in the most unintended and serendipitous fashion. Although Lorenzo "Coach" Rodriguez and I have only known each other since July of 2017, our eventual collaboration to write his autobiography had its actual birthing, unbeknownst to us, many years before.

As a young man living in Southside Montebello, California, in 1970–71, I had dabbled in the Korean martial art, hapkido, for a few short months before the Sifu (Master) suddenly closed shop and left. I had a part-time job as a janitor for a beauty salon that paid me $10 a week for one hour of work each day. I had just paid a hard-earned $20 for the month to Sifu when he suddenly left town the following day. It dawned on me after returning to the dojo each afternoon that the Sifu was never going to return. I was angry. I had been ripped off. As I was walking home on Beverly Blvd, on the northside of Montebello, I saw a flyer posted on the YWCA building entrance that read, "LimaLama Martial Arts $10 a month."

I asked myself, *LimaLama? What is that?* Curious, I walked in and found about 10 students practicing a martial art, I learned years later, was still in its infancy. LimaLama was only five years old. The instructor stood about five feet, five inches, at best. I thought he looked too young and not very muscular to be teaching a martial art. He caught my eye as I watched the class practice striking movements from a horse stance.

"Hi, I'm Master Nuñez. Are you interested in taking my LimaLama class, young man?"

Still fuming about having my money stolen from the other martial arts master, I boldly queried this instructor, "I never heard of LimaLama. How do I know it's any good?"

I was about three inches taller than him and probably outweighed him by 20 pounds. I wasn't thinking I could take him on in a fight, but I wanted to be sure that this weird sounding martial art style was real. I was incredibly fast, or so I thought, at the age of seventeen, but had no real power behind my punches. In fact, I used to carry a small solid steel pipe in my pocket, in case I got into a fight. It gave my fist more weight and power and was easily concealed in my hand. I admit, I was always fearful of fighting; but living in Los Angeles, you don't have that choice as a teenager. So, I was always mentally prepared for it.

The master looked me over and said, "Okay, I'll tell you what. Go ahead, hit, or kick me as hard and fast as you can." He lifted his right hand, showing me his palm, "I will only use this one hand. If you are able to hit or kick any part of my body, then you don't have to pay me for lessons the first month."

Foolishly, my first thought was, *I don't want to hit this guy. But I'll take the free lessons.* I asked, "Really? You want me to hit and kick you."

He calmly nodded his head, smiling.

You can guess the outcome. We were arm's length away when I started throwing punches as fast as I could. I even attempted a front kick. Predictably, he was too fast. I couldn't even see his hand movement but could feel it. He smashed his right-hand palm off both my arms with every combination I attempted and blocked my leg kick while simultaneously slapping me in the face with either side of his hand as he easily blocked my strikes. He used only one hand in humiliating me in front of his students. I never touched him but felt the power of his strikes on my arms and leg and face. After a mere five to six seconds of pain, I backed up, my hands in the air, defeated. "I'm done. I get it, sir. I want to take lessons from you." My arms and leg were pulsating with pain from his open-hand slaps and strikes, and my face was red from embarrassment.

He studied me for a second and spoke softly, "Okay, just remember this: Don't ever challenge me again, or I will hurt you." I nodded in agreement.

I lasted only a few months training under Master Richard Nuñez, as I soon ran out of money to pay for my lessons. I could have continued, but at my age I preferred to spend what little money I had on girlfriends. That was one of many shortsighted decisions I would make in life. Not until 50 years later, after my book interview sessions began with Coach, did I discover that Master Nuñez was one of the *Original Five* LimaLama masters who studied under the Great-Grandmaster (GGM), Tino Tuiolosega.

Although my experience training in LimaLama was short lived, it left a marked impression on me for years to come. The whipping or slapping-hands aspect was forever a part of my psyche when watching martial arts fights and later mixed martial arts (MMA). I practiced every day in our apartment driveway. Out of sight of anyone, I repeated over and over every form I was being taught. Even though my LimaLama training was short lived, it saved my butt a few times on the street and when I worked in the California prisons. I don't pretend to have any martial arts knowledge, but I do have an acute street awareness, having been raised in Los Angeles and later working in law enforcement.

I was unaware that, during the same time period in 1970, Coach, a mere four months my elder, had been training in El Monte, California. GM Richard Nuñez was also one of his early instructors. Fast forward 47 years to 2017, as I walked past an old winery Tasting Room in Rancho Cucamonga, I caught sight of a flyer posted on the front door and realized it was being used as a Muay Thai martial arts training room. The flyer described the instructor as an "8th Degree black belt in LimaLama." I had not seen or heard of any LimaLama studios in years. My curiosity drove me to go inside and observe the training. Coach had some students training, and three of them were young children.

When Coach introduced himself, I asked about the training approach, schedule, and age requirements. He impressed me as personable, with a relaxed demeanor. He was knowledgeable about boxing and martial arts. I immediately signed up my two male grandchildren, ages three and four, into his Mighty Mites program. I wanted them to learn martial arts. For the next year, the boys would train in Muay Thai. Coach allowed me to practice, without charge, using his equipment. I'd hit the body and punching bags as I waited for my grandchildren's practice to conclude.

I soon recruited three other family members to join in the Muay Thai training to augment their law enforcement careers. The more Coach and I talked, the more interested I became in his story. I suggested that he should write a book. I convinced him that his story was worth sharing. He had read my nonfiction book about cops, criminals, and crime, *10-33 On The West Yard*, and realized his story could really become a book. It was 2017 when Coach agreed to the book project, but he was clear about his desires. He wanted more than just a story about

INTRODUCTION 5

himself. He wanted to honor LimaLama and the martial arts community that had been a large part of his life. I happily concurred.

This book is a journey about a martial arts fighter. It introduces California martial arts history to the general public. For martial arts masters, it will remind them of the dynamic arrival of karate and kung fu in the United States. The classic forms and styles of the traditional martial arts that began their hybridization during the '60s and '70s. The blending of familiar Japanese, Pacific Island, and Chinese fighting styles merging from communities in Hawaii, like *Kajukenbo*, found welcome homes along the coastal communities of California. This was the world that Coach was introduced to when he began his formal LimaLama training.

You will read familiar names in martial arts, like Bruce Lee, Ed Parker, and Chuck Norris, all black belts in the traditional styles of Wing Chung, Kenpo, and Tang Soo Do, respectively. Each of these Grandmasters (GMs) was searching for more effective fighting methods for self-defense and tournament matches, especially when full-contact karate became more popular. These same martial arts legends soon began incorporating new techniques from other martial arts (kung fu, karate, boxing, jiu-jitsu, and judo to name a few) ultimately creating their own unique styles. It's been said that these hybrid styles were the foundation for the beginnings of mixed martial arts (MMA).

Bruce Lee created Jeet Kune Do, Ed Parker created American Kenpo Karate, and Chuck Norris created, Chun Kuk Do (Chuck Norris System). Similarly, GM Tino Tuiolosega created his own martial art style. He incorporated techniques from Samoan Lua, boxing from the Marine Corps, American Kenpo with Ed

Parker, and kung fu with Ark Yuey Wong. GM Tino ultimately created his own hybrid style of fighting called LimaLama. He translated it as *Hands of Wisdom*.

These hybrid martial arts, created in the United States, demanded the same thing—constant improvement. From these martial arts legends, techniques of fighting were meant to continue to grow and evolve. That is the martial arts legacy Coach Rodriguez has continued to follow and teach with his students, but always honoring his LimaLama roots.

―――――◆―――――

The book is arranged into six distinct Chapters. **Chapter 1**, The Origins of LimaLama, introduces the remarkable history of GGM Tu'umanmao "Tino" Tuiolosega. What he learned under the two principal Grandmasters heavily influenced the martial art he eventually created.

Chapter 2, The Birth of a Warrior, describes the life of Coach Rodriguez, from his birth in Mexico to the family's journey to southern California and then to Coach's unique introduction and training in LimaLama.

Chapter 3, Honing the Sword, and **Chapter 4**, Becoming a Champion, provide insight into the making of a highly skilled fighter in street brawls, unsanctioned fights, and ultimately to the kickboxing circuit and eventual champion.

Chapter 5, The Next Generation, provides us with a look into the culture and politics of martial arts, as well as Coach Rodriguez's experience in training fighters for championships and his years promoting kickboxing tournaments. The chapter shares his transition from fighter to trainer and promoter. And some of the interesting students he guided to championships.

Chapter 6, Mixed Martial Arts, is where Coach shares his journey into the world of MMA, the fighters he trained, and his experience as a professional Cutman. He concludes the chapter introducing the grandmaster who brought LimaLama to the forefront in Mexico and Latino America, where it continues to thrive today with well over 100,000 practitioners.

Finally, in the **Epilogue**, Coach Rodriguez shares his vision on fighting, the state of martial arts training today, and his hope for future generations of students, black belts, and masters.

Coach is unique among his LimaLama peers. First, he had no other formal fight training before becoming a student under Master Sal Esquival and GM Tino. Secondly, from the streets to military service, underground fights, to full-contact karate and kickboxing tournaments, he used his fighting skills to prevail. Thus, his eventual achievement in becoming a black belt was not restricted to simply dojo kata training and testing. Third, his formal training in boxing, Ba Gua and kickboxing started after he joined the Army, which reinforced his belief about the fighting arts being fluid and not constrained.

Our friendship grew closer over the years in our interview sessions. I always recorded our lunch visits and observed his quiet but confident demeanor. He never spoke with an egotistic breath when sharing his stories. On the contrary, I continually had to pull from him details on the *who, what, when, why, and how* of all his amazing fight encounters. He never seemed impressed with himself. I continually pushed the question about the many skirmishes he had. "Coach, why did you do that?"

More often than not, he'd matter-of-factly respond, "I don't like bullies." Or he'd say, "I wanted to test my training."

Coach Rodriguez, like most martial artists, is capable of killing someone in a fight. Fortunately, that has never happened. Instead, as you will read, he inflicted great bodily injury with reason and purpose. He readily admits that when he fought, he had "bad intentions" because he assumed his street adversary or ring opponent had the same intentions too. He never wanted to lose a fight, in or out of the ring. Even when he was angry, he intended to hurt his enemy combatant, but he stopped once they gave up or were unconscious. This is exactly what martial arts masters are: in control of themselves to control the situation.

His real-life *fighting* experiences were no big deal to him; he thought they were *normal*. For him they were normal because he fought so often. He was merely responding to the circumstances in front of him. For the rest of us, many of those events are surreal. And, only a few are highlighted in the book as examples of the hundreds of fights he actually had. So join me as we read about the life and times of a great martial artist who truly can be called a LimaLama Warrior.

Richard Alvarado
Founder/Editor-In-Chief, Órale Press

1
THE ORIGINS OF LIMALAMA

THE GRANDMASTER

TU'UMAMAO "TINO" TUIOLOSEGA, GRAND MASTER (GM) and Founder of *LimaLama, Art of Self-Defense,* is both a legend and somewhat of a mystery to much of the martial arts world. This much is sure: he was respected among a core of American martial artist legends he encountered during the '50s, '60s, and '70s. He was also feared by those he didn't like, and for good reason. In his youth, he was a ruthless street fighter. As an adult martial artist, he was deadly. The following is a summary of what could be found about this great martial artist and what is known about him from people who knew him as students, peers, and/or adversaries.

Tino was born in Tutuila, (Pago Pago), American Samoa, on July 2, 1931, son of Tu'umamao Tuiolosega, tribal leader of the island of Olosega and Sapsapoaluga Feagaimaleata Poumele Tuiolosega. The last name Tuiolosega literally means "King of Olosega." Tino was never a king, and his family never claimed to be heirs to a kingdom, but it is agreed that he came from tribal *Olosega* blood and that Tino's father was considered a high chief of his clan. Among the island tribes throughout the

Pacific, warrior and healer elders were considered to be island royalty who traditionally guided tribal life. Tino's father was also a court judge on the island and held influence as a chief among his family and local community.

An example of the Tuiolosega family status in Samoa was the time Tino visited the island to attend a family wedding. All the local chiefs showed up. One chief arrived that had not been invited. Because there was no handwoven ceremonial mat for him, the wedding was almost canceled. By tradition, each chief had their own ceremonial mat. Tino was willing to give the chief his mat to use, but it would have been considered an insult to the chief to accept and a dishonor to the Tuiolosega family to be considered less than the other chief. The rich traditions of the island overruled all other considerations. Fortunately, a mat was soon located and brought to the wedding.

The Pacific Ocean is the location of a wide variety of small islands ranging from Hawaii off the west coast of the Americas to the Philippines. In between lay Samoa, Guam, the Cook Islands, Tonga, and others. These islands are generally considered to be part of the *Polynesian Triangle*, which stretches from Hawaii to Easter Island to New Zealand. Historically, these islands have been home to unique tribal cultures and as such, have birthed some of the most effective war arts. Many of these arts evolved in a vacuum—untouched by other cultures—and contained their own unique tactics, weaponry, and methodology.

As the son of Samoan royal heritage, Tino was required to learn numerous Polynesian movements of fighting from both his father and his uncle. Tino's position in his family line carried with it great responsibility because the movements he learned were restricted by sect and family lineage. What he was taught was considered sacred and was passed onto descendants of the island tribal families only by fathers or immediate relatives. His uncle, who was considered a major influence in his fighting exercises, worked extensively with him in giving him an understanding the concepts of these movements.

The history of Tongan and Samoan fighting styles is recorded by many captains of the European ships that landed on the islands, noting the skilled boxing and wrestling acumen of the tribes. The island tribes had, by necessity, learned to master fighting techniques to protect themselves from becoming slaves or from being vanquished from their island homes by other tribes. Eventually, Christianity was forced upon the islands, and the brutality of the Polynesian fighting styles was outlawed as a means to pacify the villagers. The recorded history of Polynesian fighting styles became footnotes from European invaders ship records and only passed on secretly through tribal oral history and practice.

BIRTH OF A SAMOAN WARRIOR

Many of the early movements that would become the foundation for LimaLama were actually concealed in the island dances during the 1800s, due to both political and religious pressure which resulted in banning the open teaching of the Polynesian deadly arts. Instead, the movements were hidden within the hula and other Polynesian sword and weapon dances where they remained alive, to those in the know, who were able to decode the graceful, flowing movements of the dance.

A hula flowing hand movement is actually demonstrated in LimaLama's salutation that Tino first created. Unlike most martial arts salutations, LimaLama's salute has no bow. In Tino's world, "LimaLama does not bow to any man, only to god." At the core of LimaLama's flowing tactics lie a series of methods which translate ancient tribal bone locking and breaking techniques, vital pressure point and killing methods derived from Samoan and other Polynesian arts believed to be representative of those used by Pacific Island warriors centuries ago.

An athletic and daring Tino joined the US Marine Corps at the age of seventeen in 1947 and participated in the *Inchon Landing* in Korea. The Battle of Inchon was an amphibious invasion and a battle of the Korean War that resulted in a decisive victory and strategic reversal in favor of the United Nations Command. Tino was cited and decorated for his actions in that battle. Tino's exceptional fighting skill, speed, and veracity soon led to his becoming a chief instructor in hand-to-hand combat training for the Marines and Naval personnel after his wartime mission.

He also participated in boxing and judo events while serving in the military. As an amateur boxer, he fought over 135 fights, winning 108 by knockout. Some of his titles included All Pacific Inter-School Boxing Conference, All Far East, All Pacific Inter-Service, All Armed Forces, Pan Pacific, All Maritime, Fourteen Naval District, AAU, and Eleventh District Championships. He was honorably discharged from military service in 1955.

TINO'S FORMAL MARTIAL ARTS TRAINING

Tino met his future wife, Claire, in 1952, and by 1956 they had three children. To earn extra money, he entertained vacationers at local beach hotels as a Hawaiian knife and fire dancer. In 1956, Tino and his family moved to California looking for work when he became aware of Ed Parker's Kenpo Karate studio in Pasadena. Coincidently, GM Parker's father was the minister who had married Clair and Tino in Hawaii. GM Parker soon realized the innate fighting abilities of his prized student, and within two years Tino had reached the brown belt level in American Kenpo Karate, even though his fighting skills were already beyond that level.

GM Parker routinely tasked Tino to teach other students, including black belt students, during the same period. There is no documented information regarding when or if Tino received his black belt in Kenpo Karate, but it is believed that Tino preferred to wear the brown belt to catch other martial artists off guard. Besides, it didn't matter to him what belt color he or others held to distinguish skill set. What mattered most to him was, could they fight?

Tino was one of the most infamous fighters of karate matches held *within* martial arts schools and dojos. Occasionally, Tino would drop by the Pasadena school and workout with Grandmaster Ed Parker and anyone else who would get on the mat with him. Students who saw him fight, agreed that Tino could easily defeat anyone in the school or in an exhibition. They were in awe of his exceptional fighting prowess.

Open karate competition tournaments did not yet exist. Even when Tino did compete in tournaments, he fought to crush his opponent, not to score points. He was routinely disqualified for strikes to the face. This would become a similar pattern followed by the first generation of his future LimaLama masters. Most of the old practitioners and masters from that period in California still recall "Mr. Tino" as one of the most feared martial artists of his time.

Tino was routinely used by GM Parker to respond to challenges made by competing schools. Tino would play with his opponent; but if the sparring got serious, he would "put him in his place with a beating." Master Sal Esquivel shared the story about a US Marine who came into the Parker school and challenged one of the black belts in the gym. Tino, wearing his familiar brown belt, went after the guy and began beating the guy up badly. To everyone watching, it looked like Tino was trying to kill him. The marine ran out of the building, and Tino went after him. It took six students to grab and sit on Tino, holding him down until he cooled off.

Another time, I witnessed a black belt approach Tino at a tournament and say something that angered him. Without hesitation, Tino slapped the black belt, who stood in shocked amazement. The assault was viewed by all in attendance. The black belt never saw the strike coming. He didn't do anything in response as Tino stood at arm's length, staring at him. The embarrassed black belt quickly exited the venue, never to return.

During this period, in the late '50s and early '60s, GM Parker created the Kenpo organization. Tino was asked by Ed Parker to visit other schools and recruit them for the new Kenpo organization. Tino would go out and secure various schools in southern California to join the new Kenpo Karate Association. No one would bad-mouth or refuse to join when approached by Tino. It was typical of him to let his fists do the talking if he felt a black belt school owner was being disrespectful. The word quickly got around the martial arts community not to mess with "Mr. Tino."

In or about 1960, Tino was introduced by his friend, Haumea "Tiny" Lefiti, to Grandmaster (GM) Ark Yuey Wong. GM Wong was a Registered Master Sipak of the Five Families or Ancestors and Sil-Lum (Five Animals). Tino was like a sponge as a kung fu student. He quickly memorized and performed every move. GM Wong was so impressed with Tino's fighting ability and learning skills that he brought in kung fu masters from different styles to teach him. GM Tino was conferred a master's degree in the Five Animals and Five Family styles of kung fu from Grandmaster Wong. At the time, it is believed Tino was the first non-Asian in over 85 years to achieve such an honor.

THE ORIGINS OF LIMALAMA

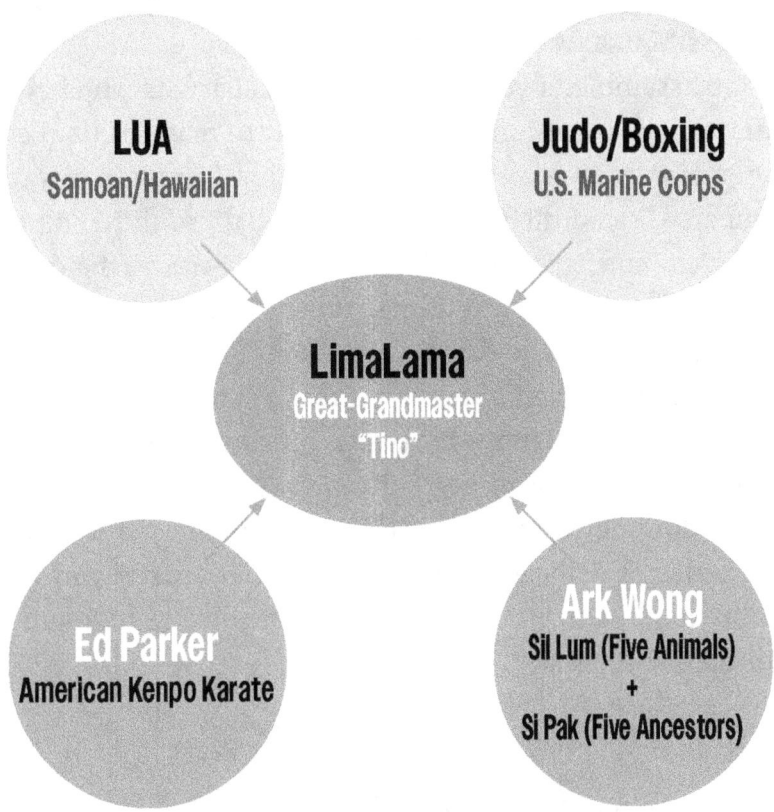

The martial arts lineage of LimaLama.

BIRTH OF LIMALAMA

By 1965, Tino was ready to introduce his own hybrid martial art style. While living in San Gabriel, California, he decided to call his fighting style *LimaLama*. The word *LimaLama* is a blending of the Samoan language words, *lima* (hand) and *malamalama* (understanding). Tuiolosega defined LimaLama to mean "knowledge and understanding," and translated it as "Hands of wisdom." His new martial art style was a mix of Samoan street fighting, Kenpo Karate, Chinese kung fu, nearly every Japanese martial art, American boxing, and wrestling. His credo: Always move forward, "LimaLama doesn't back up."

Always attack, "LimaLama doesn't defend." And always finish the fight, "LimaLama doesn't forgive."

Tino assembled five committed martial artists who had the dedication, courage, and requisite skills to master LimaLama. Under his tutelage, the five original LimaLama organization members—Richard Nuñez, John Louis, Sal Esquivel, Solomon Kaihewalu and Haumea F. "Tiny" Lefiti—became the driving influence for establishing LimaLama as a force in the martial arts community. Tino knew the original five members were all alpha-male personalities and already accomplished martial arts fighters. GM Tino was trying to bring a new martial art into the world and wanted gladiators who could represent the art in a dominating fashion. GM Tino's intent was to create a loyal cadre of dedicated and fierce martial artists who could comprehend his techniques and garner a strong following of dedicated students.

THE ORIGINS OF LIMALAMA

ESTABLISHING THE TILOA

There is no historical dispute that GM Tino created the name and formed the organization that became known as *Tuiolosega International LimaLama Organization & Associations* (TILOA). Although much has been written about the "Original Six" members and their contributions as the first LimaLama Warriors, the truth is that the five warriors (listed below) were black belt masters under GM Tino. The original five were already accomplished martial artists, but none of them could match GM Tino's fighting knowledge, skills, or ability. They left their martial art styles because they knew that LimaLama was a lethal martial art that combined the best of other fighting systems. They wanted to master the flowing hands and whipping palm techniques that GM Tino used so effectively.

Here is a brief biography of the first five LimaLama practitioners who established the TILOA:

Haumea F. "Tiny" Lefiti was a giant Samoan martial artist born in Hawaii in 1930. He weighed over 325 pounds and was well over six feet tall. Tiny had a background in boxing, including Golden Gloves and semi-pro matches. He had a storied history of Samoan and Hawaiian street and knife fighting. (It has been said that Tiny's favorite weapon was the straight razor.) During his tour of duty with the Marine Corps, Tiny was a drill instructor and Special Forces soldier. He trained in Japanese karate for over five years while stationed in Japan, reaching the rank of 2nd degree black belt. Later, while stationed in Taiwan, during two years with a Nationalist Chinese general, he was trained in Mok Ga style of kung fu, also known as Monk's Style or Monk Fist Boxing (Lohan Chuan).

Upon Tiny's return to the United States, the general gave him a letter of introduction to the only teacher of Mok Ga known in the United States at the time, Grandmaster Ark Yuey Wong of Los Angeles, California. Tiny began training with the late Master Ralph Shun, Ark Wong's most senior student and disciple. He received his black belt from Master Shun and then began private lessons with Grandmaster Wong. He learned the major forms from the Five Families style and Five Animals styles. During the early '60s, Tiny had introduced his close friend Tino Tuiolosega to GM Wong. Tiny passed away in February of 1973 from a heart attack at the young age of 43.

Solomon Kaihewalu was born on December 2, 1935. He started his karate training under Master John Louis (an American kickboxer, point karate fighter and actor), in the Okinawa-Te system. Solomon is the only original LimaLama master who didn't have a black belt prior to studying under GM Tino. Tino was very protective of his new LimaLama martial arts system but recognized Solomon's superior fighting skills and dedication. A year later, GM Tino awarded Solomon his LimaLama black belt. Solomon eventually moved back to Hawaii and created his own fighting system called the *Hawaiian Martial Art of Kaihewalu Ohana Lua*.

John Louis was a Black Belt in the Okinawa Te karate under Master Gordon Doversola. He served in the United States Army during the Korean conflict and had instructor ratings in Kendo, Kenpo, jiu-jitsu, and kung-fu. He recognized the special qualities of LimaLama and eventually received a black belt in LimaLama under GM Tino.

Richard Nuñez was born in East Los Angeles in 1930. He was the smallest of the original LimaLama masters, standing five foot seven and weighing around 140 pounds. He studied boxing before his formal martial arts training in Kajukenbo under Grandmaster Dan Guzman. Master Nuñez had his own school when he was visited by GM Tino.

Tino had been organizing martial arts schools under Ed Parker's Karate Association and intended for the Nuñez school to join the association or close its doors. When confronted with

THE ORIGINS OF LIMALAMA

the untenable option, it is said that Master Nuñez looked Tino in the eye and said, "Well, if that's the way it has to be, then let's do this."

Master Nuñez took a fighting stance against Tino. Tino smiled, appreciating Master Nunez's courage and resolve not to submit and said, "I like you. You can stay."

Master Nuñez, known for his fast hands and agile footwork, had seen Tino compete at tournaments. He knew Tino was too fast and powerful and had beaten black belts easily in and outside tournament events. He realized there was much more to this martial art, and he wanted to learn Tino's hand movements. Master Nuñez became one of the original masters of LimaLama, and he is one of the key reasons LimaLama schools flourished in Mexico.

Sal Esquivel was a competitive body builder residing in El Monte, California, when he began his martial arts studies in Kajukenbo under Grandmaster Dan Guzman. Despite his five foot seven, 190-pound frame, he was in peak physical condition and a fierce competitor in the ring or in a street fight. He was a straightforward fighter in tournaments and known to never back down from anyone.

Master Sal's first impression of LimaLama came from a tournament bout against GM Tino which Master Sal won. GM Rigoberto Lopez shared the story of how Master Sal met GM Tino. Master Sal won the match because GM Tino was disqualified for hitting Master Sal in the head, nearly knocking him out. GM Lopez observed that GM Tino's speed was too fast and his strikes much harder than Master Sal's. Master Sal realized that GM Tino was playing with him on the mat. He knew that he was no match for GM Tino. That was enough to convince Master Sal that this unknown martial art was what he wanted to learn. He became one of the original five LimaLama masters and helped advance the art in Latin America.

MEMBERS OF THE FIRST LIMALAMA ASSOCIATION

Richard Nunez, John Maroll, Sal Esquivel, Solomon Kaihewalu, Grand Master Tino Tuiolosega, Huumea 'Tiny' Lafiti

GREAT-GRANDMASTER TINO TUIOLOSEGA

The Original Five

| Master Tiny Lefiti | Master Richard Nuñez | Master Sal Esquivel | Master John Louis | Master Solomon Kaihewalu |

The 1st Generation

| Marry Manuga | George Malifua | Don Lombardo | Rigoberto Lopez | Ted Tabura | Lorenzo Rodriguez | Gary Knutson | Al Garza Sr. | Dan Mitchell |

It didn't take long for LimaLama to get noticed at tournaments or dojo sparring exhibitions. Few competitors came close to defeating TILOA LimaLama students. LimaLama students were typically more aggressive and effective strikers. GGM Tino and the original five expected their students to be the toughest of the tough in any martial arts circle. If they lost a fight, then the TILOA would lose too, and that was unacceptable to GGM Tino. Richard Nuñez and Sal Esquival would ultimately introduce LimaLama to generations of Latinos from South Central Los Angeles, East Los Angeles, the San Gabriel Valley, and eventually to Latin America and beyond.

In the '70s, the TILOA was involved with both martial artists and professional full-contact training of fighters who wished to compete in the professional ranks. It grew during the 80's and 90's under the tutelage of the first generation LimaLama masters. Today LimaLama has its largest concentration of schools in Mexico, South and Central America, Germany, and Spain. Others are found throughout the United States, especially in California and Hawaii, and as far away as Australia. GGM Tino also acted as technical advisor/choreographer on several TV series and did an action film called *Seven* with several of his close martial arts friends, Ed Parker, and Tadashi Yamashita.

GM Tino was close to many known grandmasters and masters in the martial arts world, among them Bruce Lee, Chuck Norris, Jimmy Woo, Ed Parker, and Dan Guzman. He also certified many popular black belts, among them Benny "The Jet" Urquidez, Rigoberto "Father of LimaLama in Mexico" Lopez, Ted Tabura, and many more.

GM Tino died at the age of 79 in Santa Cruz with his family at his bedside on March 22, 2011.

2
THE BIRTH OF A WARRIOR

"CURTIDOR"

MY LIFE BEGAN, LIKE most people who come to the United States, from humble beginnings. I was born in Mexico, Teocaltiche, Jalisco, on February 12, 1955. My father, Lorenzo E. Rodriguez, and mother, Maria Dolores Lopez Rodriguez, had five children. My older brother, Hector Rodriguez, my sister Leticia Rodriguez, and twin boys Luis Humberto Rodriguez and me. Many years later, another little brother, Armando Ruben Rodriguez, arrived. We weren't expecting him, and I suspect, neither were my parents.

I was born in the house that we lived in, and I was the smaller of the twins. I wasn't the first born, I was the second, and my twin brother, Luis Humberto, was said to be big and healthy. I was so small when I was born that they put me in a shoebox and put me inside an open drawer, which was my first crib.

My dad figured, since we were twins, to name one of the twins Lorenzo. And, as I was told many times later as a teenager, jokingly, my mom was known to have said, "Name the little guy over there. He's probably going to die anyway."

My dad, because of tradition, had originally wanted to name my twin brother, the first born, Lorenzo, but my uncle said,

"No, no, no, you're not going to name him Lorenzo. If you do, people are going to call all your children, 'the Lenchos.'" Sometimes, it seems the tradition of giving nicknames to families and people was created just to tease each other.

A funny Mexican tradition about nicknames. Once you get tagged, it becomes your moniker for life. Some are familiar, like "Beto" for Humberto. Some are based on appearance, like "Pecas" for freckles or spots on your face. In my grandfather's family, there were eleven children, and his first name was Preciaño. My oldest uncle was also Preciaño. They all were called the "Chayanos." My father wisely decided to name my twin older brother Luis Humberto. But he chose to name me, the second born twin, Lorenzo Enrique Jr. My brother, Luis, died when I was about six months old. Everyone had thought I wouldn't survive, because I was so small, but I had beaten the odds. I didn't know it then, but I had won my first fight--the fight for life.

My brother Luis Humberto may have left this world, but sometimes I see and feel his presence around me. Even my parents would tell me that I often carried a conversation with someone only I could see. When I was bathing and they tried to get me out, I would say, "No, Luis isn't done yet." If we were at the store and my mother was going to buy me a toy, I would tell her to buy two. Most of the time she wouldn't do it, and I would make a big fuss that she needed to buy two toys. She knew what I was feeling—that Luis wanted one too—so sometimes she would buy two toys.

We come from a hard-working family called "Curtidors." A curtidor cut and purified cow hides for leather work. The Curtidor's' job was to take the hair off cow hides and prepare the skins for use. Humans have been tanning hides to make leather since prehistoric times, using them for clothing and shelter. Byproducts of the cattle carcass, such as bones, blood,

THE BIRTH OF A WARRIOR

and fat, end up in soap, fertilizer, gelatin, medicines, and other products. But leather has always been the most valued byproduct of the cow.

My grandfather, Preciaño Rodriguez, was renowned in Jalisco for tanning the raw steer hides. He would dig big holes in the floor and put corrosive chemicals in the formed pit. He then threw the cow hides in the pit and mashed them. He would painstakingly dehair, degrease, and desalt the hides to remove any remaining hair and residue. He literally jumped in the hole wearing only pants cut off at the knees. With a large mashing tool, he'd stomp and stir the hides to remove the hair. The process was grimy and dirty, but his work resulted in a clean and beautiful hide. You could tell which guys in town were Curtidors because they had no hair on their legs below the knee. People came from all over Mexico, and they would visit my grandfather, because he was so good at prepping the hides for leathermakers to use.

That may be one of the reasons my father had originally come to the United States—for work—to improve our lives. My Uncle Pablo "Nacho" Rodriguez was living in Los Angeles, and he had asked my dad to come work in the United States. My father was already working in Los Angeles before I was born. I guess neither man wanted to lose the hair off his legs.

My mom didn't want us to be Curtidors either. My father had sent money to my mother to open a little store to help support the family, but I was too young to understand and realize they were always working. Later, my father was able to bring us all across the border to East Los Angeles. Looking back, I realize what a hard life it was for my parents in Mexico. I am grateful for their decision to come to the United States. In a sense, my parents were Curtidors as my brothers and sister would become the Lorenzo *family hides*, taking shape in a new land.

L–R: Hector, Lorenzo "Lencho," and Leticia "Letty" Rodriguez, about 1963.

EAST LOS ANGELES

It was 1958 and I was three years old when I came to live in Los Angeles, California. Looking back, my Uncle Nacho kind of reminded me of the character Fonzie from the TV program, *Happy Days*. He was an original L.A. pachuco. He always had the best clothes, the best car, the best shoes, and stuff like that. He wasn't into the gang life. He wasn't into the zoot-suit craze either. But back then, he was just a pachuco, it wasn't his style to follow the crowd. Tio Nacho was his own man.

We grew up first, in East Los Angeles, by Olympic Boulevard, about ten minutes from the old Sears building. We used to visit Sears every year about two weeks before we started school. My Mom would take us down to the basement, to the catalog department, and order all our shoes. She'd order only the wing-tipped shoes because they lasted forever. So that was our thing.

THE BIRTH OF A WARRIOR

Sears became our local landmark. Anytime we got lost, all my brothers and sister, everyone knew to look for that tall Sears building. If we were lost, Sears would point us in the right direction to get home.

I attended Saint Turibius Church and School. It was a mission belonging to St. Joseph's Parish. The Franciscan Missionary Sisters of the Immaculate Conception opened the school on September 11, 1949. In 1960, the Franciscan Missionary Sisters withdrew from Saint Turibius School, and the school welcomed the Franciscan Sisters of Penance and Christian Charity. I hated it.

I hated it because the church wanted all the students to speak only English. I remember this guy wanted to use the bathroom, but he didn't know how to ask in English. The nuns were too strict. He kept asking in Spanish, "Por favor, necesito usar el baño." (Please, I have to use the bathroom.) The nun would ignore him or yell at him to speak English. I felt bad for him. He eventually peed in class, and they made him wear a towel robe and sit on a bench during recess.

I know he felt humiliated. It happened to a lot of the kids. I also knew that wasn't going to happen to me. I spoke English. But even if I couldn't speak English, I would have just walked out of class if I needed to use the bathroom badly. I wasn't going to allow the nuns to embarrass me like they did other students. Looking back, I see now that my stubborn pride, to not accept any threat or any insult, would be the beginning of my untold destiny.

A lot of the kids in class would have an accident and pee in their pants, and instead of the sisters teaching them proper English, they would punish them. What's worse, many of us weren't allowed to speak English at home. So, here was my dilemma. I couldn't speak Spanish at school, and I wasn't allowed to speak English at my house! My parents did it so that we wouldn't forget our native tongue. But it was hard. My little brother didn't have it as bad as the rest of us children because, by the time he was born, we already spoke English fluently. The bad thing about it today is that a lot of my nieces, even my daughter, don't speak fluent Spanish. You know they understand the language, but it's kind of sad they don't practice.

Both my parents worked. Back then, we didn't know what a *latchkey kid* meant, but that was us: stay-at-home-alone kids while the parents worked. Like the majority of Latinos today, my parents came to the United States to work. They would take whatever job they could get. Luckily, my Uncle Nacho helped them out.

The house that we lived in reminded me of the *Addams Family* house we saw on TV. It had six or seven bedrooms and a basement. A lot of my friends would visit me but wouldn't go into the house. They said that the house was haunted. We never saw any ghosts, so we didn't care.

The house that we lived in was so big that everybody would come, and sometimes it seemed they would never leave. Brothers, uncles, acquaintances, came to that house, sometimes staying two or three years. The house was so big, it never felt crowded. The house no longer exists. The state tore it down when they built the 110 Freeway. I recall the front yard had a gigantic avocado tree. I hated that tree. Every time I raked up leaves, it seemed to take forever. And by the time I finished, more leaves had fallen. I recall when the State of California was building the 110 freeway, I would grab the biggest avocados and toss them up onto the freeway. I could hear them pop; then all of a sudden, I would hear somebody cussing me out from above. I would run and hide. It was fun.

My parents seemed to be always working. As children, we never realized that they both had gone straight from secondary school to working full time in Mexico. Since our parents both

THE BIRTH OF A WARRIOR

worked, we did a few chores, but not many. Mostly, we played outside or watched TV until they got home. Then my mom would cook dinner, wash clothes, and iron. That's the way it was in our home: we had a supermom and didn't really appreciate her sacrifices until we became adults.

I recall my dad worked at a painting company when he first came to the United States. I'm not sure if my dad came to this side of the border with papers, legally. I don't know how he crossed. My parents never said anything about it. My mom worked in a factory during this time in my life. On the weekends, we used to drive to Compton. We had family there, our compadres (godparents). That's when there were a lot more Mexicans from Latin America than any other group living in Compton. We'd practically spend the whole weekend there. That's how my parents were, they worked hard and partied hard too. In my youth, it was something I took for granted.

My uncle Nacho wanted to join the Navy, but the Navy wouldn't let him in because he wasn't a United States citizen. He always had the goal of going into the Navy. But that didn't end his dream of being on the water. He ended up buying a boat, plus scuba and fishing gear, to fill that need. It was a really big deal for us and those who knew him. He had all my uncles and primos (cousins) working for him to catch fish to sell. Better than that, he'd take us kids to go deep sea fishing too.

I remember one time when we were little, all our cousins and friends came over to the house. Everybody was playing hide-and-go-seek, and I wanted to play, but I was too little. I was only about five years old. My sister and brother told me to go into the house. I got mad and took off running. I ended up on a busy business street. These two sailors found me, and they went door to door until they found my parents. When asked what I was doing on the road, I said, "I went out because I wanted to buy shoes." The truth was, I just wanted to play hide-and-go-seek. I didn't know where everybody was, so I kept walking and walking and got lost.

As soon as the sailors left, my dad took hold of my older brother Hector and my sister and spanked them. Then it was my turn. Yeah, he gave me a spanking, but I didn't mind it because I was more scared about being out there in the streets by myself. My brothers and sisters never let me forget that silly episode in my life—getting lost on a busy street. They always bring it up, and we still laugh about it.

Right before we left East Los Angeles in 1961, my brother Hector got jumped by a gang in L.A. I don't remember the name of the gang. We were in Catholic school, and I was six years old in first grade. My older brother was a good soccer player. They called him "El Torito" (the little bull). He was quick and tough like a bull. I don't know why they were trying to beat him up. When I saw him being attacked by some guys, I ran over and started swinging at them and bit one guy on the leg. Hector got mad at me for joining in the fight. But, in my mind, that was my brother—I wouldn't hesitate to try to help him.

I didn't realize it then, but that was one of many more fights I would have in my life. On reflection, it showed my instinct to want to fight without a care for the consequences. It was a trait that was clearly a double-edged sword in my life too. Anyway, about a week or two after that, we moved to La Verne. I'm not sure why, but I guess because of the gang presence, our parents moved us to La Verne. I was barely on my way into second grade in public school.

LA VERNE

My parents weren't strict. They gave us a few chores but not many house rules. But they didn't hesitate to put us in our place if we misbehaved. If we did something wrong, my mom would give us a butt spanking. Most of the time we deserved

THE BIRTH OF A WARRIOR

it. But the worst part was, as soon as she was walking out the door, she would say, "Wait until your father gets home." Oh, man, we would try to go to bed early. You know, go to bed early and pretend to sleep.

My father would come home, and mom would tell him what we did wrong. Then he would come into our room and say, "Okay, Get up. You know you're not asleep." He was intending to spank us, and we knew it. It looked like we were playing jump rope with him, as he tried to whip us. He would take his belt off and start swinging it. We looked like Mexican jumping beans, as we tried to avoid getting hit by his belt. Finally, he'd reach out and grab a hand or arm to pull us down and then whack our butts.

One time, during the summer, when the *Slip and Slide* commercial barely came out, it looked like fun. It was just a large plastic sheet about 10 feet long connected to a hose with water coursing over the top. The commercials showed kids playing, laughing, and having fun. Of course, I asked, "How come we don't have a slip and slide?" Was it because we couldn't afford it? No, it was because we didn't have a grass lawn. Our yard was all concrete. That didn't matter to us, though.

My brothers and I, being smart Mexicans, got dish soap and put it on the sidewalk. We ran water over it and went sliding. I decided to do it standing up. I slipped, and *Bam!* I hit my head! When I woke up, I found myself in bed. But what was worse, I was cross-eyed. But I wasn't worried about that. I was worried about the spanking that my mom was going to give me. And because my parents took turns punishing us, I thought, "*Now I'm done. I'm going to get hit twice!*" I guess I probably had a concussion because they never spanked me. I was a pendejo, trying to slide on soapy cement. In those days, we always had to find ways to entertain ourselves, but that sliding game definitely hurt.

We lived a couple of years in La Verne. One thing I recalled telling myself before we moved there, *If we are going to get a house, it can't have trees!* I hated raking around the old avocado tree in East LA. My demands obviously didn't matter, though. My parents rented a house that had about 15 trees—pomegranate, peaches, apples, apricots, oranges, and figs—you name it, and I had to rake them all.

And if that wasn't enough, the yard was so huge that my parents also planted corn and vegetables. My life was over, I was doomed to yard duty! The backyard even had a huge fountain, so big you could get in and practically swim. We used to go to Puddingstone Lake and snare catfish and throw them in the fountain. We had a lot of fun. My primos would come over and we told them to go swimming. We knew that the catfish would bite them. They would jump out, thinking there was a monster in there.

We lived about 30 feet from the train tracks. In the evening, we couldn't go to sleep as the trains would pass by. After a while, we got used to it. Later, as a teenager, I started telling time by the train schedules. Then I even started hitching a ride. The trains didn't move too fast. I'd jump on the train and go a couple of miles. We would hitch a ride or ride our bikes to the fairgrounds. And, at Puddingstone Park, we would go and throw our fishing lines out to try to catch some fish. And, if we caught fish, we wouldn't go to school. We would clean the fish and make a barbeque right there. Everybody brought food and drinks. I was probably 11 or 12 years old by then. My parents had everything at that house. They had all kinds of other fruit from the trees—lots of nuts and stuff like that—so we always had something to eat.

Looking back, it seemed my parents' constant work schedules made it easy for us to be more mischievous. We'd put coins, long nails, or soda cans on the train tracks and watch the trains

THE BIRTH OF A WARRIOR

pass over and flatten or blow them up. We would make bows and arrows. At night, we would go hunting. We didn't kill any dogs, but for some reason, we didn't like cats. As a result, there were no cats in our neighborhood.

We did a lot of horsing around, mostly at Bonelli Park, Puddingstone Lake. My primos in Mexico had taught my brother and me how to hunt and clean rabbits. My Uncle Manuel taught us how to fish. We would go fishing and hunting at the park. We would take bows and arrows, BB guns, and slingshots. We were good at slingshots—not those big old sling shots that they have here in the states; the small little ones you get from Mexico—and we used BBs—ball bearings. We killed rabbits and cleaned them right there at the park—taking the hide and bones out and enjoying a free meal. It was fun.

Every time we visited Mexico, it was an adventure. One day we would go hunting, another day we would go horseback riding, and the day after, we would do something else. We would go to Mexico like every other year to Teocaltiche, Jalisco. My dad drove us. My dad drove like a viejo (old man), really slow. We used to drive from El Monte to Tijuana. Even from L.A, it would take us five to six hours! He would take the slow lane and drive, drive, drive. When we got there, my dad would buy all kinds of food and arrive at my cousin's house. Man, everybody would eat!

It was customary that we'd come home on Sunday. My dad would tell everyone, "We're leaving, we have to go to work tomorrow, and the kids go to school." However, it took him forever to say goodbye. He would say, "Okay, ya nos vamos." (We're leaving now.) Another hour passed by, "Okay, ya nos vamos." And another hour passed by. By then, we would be falling asleep. When we crossed the border, we had to wake up because immigration officers would ask us, "Where are you from?" Most of the time they just let us sleep.

We passed a lot of our primos over the border that way. Many times, on purpose, my parents would tell us just to go to sleep, so that immigration wouldn't wake us up, because were passing one of our primos over to the United States. We would get home about three or four o'clock in the morning. My dad would take a shower and have some coffee and cigarettes and go straight to work. We didn't want to go to school in the morning, but we weren't given a choice.

We had an old, old, ugly green station wagon. I mean that thing was an *ugly* green. But that old wagon took us back and forth across the border all the time. I remember our first dog, her name was Muñeca (doll). She just hopped right into the car in Tijuana on one of our trips back. Muñeca jumped into the car, and we said, "Oh, you want to go? Well, you'd better be quiet."

We passed her through the border without papers, just like we would for one of our primos. When we were ready to return from Tijuana back to LA, she got in underneath the seat. No whimper, no nothing. Immigration turned around and asked us if we had anything to declare. We'd respond, "No sir, nothing. We didn't buy anything." As luck would have it, the Border Patrol officers didn't check the car and let us pass.

At home, when my dad would go to the market—he was used to going to the store every day like they do in Mexico for the newspaper—if he didn't take Muñeca with him, she would start crying. That's how close they became. When my dad would return home, Muñeca would be waiting for him at the door. She was his baby. She lived with us a long, long time. She was just a mutt. Sort of a sheepdog–cocker-spaniel mix. She gave birth to a couple of litters, and we gave the pups to our cousins and neighbors.

THE BIRTH OF A WARRIOR

SOUTH EL MONTE

My Uncle Nacho bought a house in South El Monte. And so, he started telling the family, "Compadres! Hey, come down here. It's closer to your work." My tios all worked together, so they convinced my parents to move to South El Monte. But we didn't know that there's a good life on one side of the track and a bad life on the other side of the track. We moved to the wrong side of the track in South El Monte.

But we didn't know it. For us it was a proud moment, knowing our parents were buying a new home—we thought it was great. Later, my Uncle Manuel "Tito" Rodriguez also bought a house in South El Monte. The compadres would come over, or we would go to their place just across the street. And next door, there was a big field with a big tree, I think the neighborhood called it "Mr. Mistes." Anywhere you went in El Monte, if you got lost, all you had to do was find that tree, and you knew how to get home.

We had a huge fig tree at our house, and we had a treehouse on top of it. A lot of the kids in the neighborhood wanted that treehouse. And because we were new to the neighborhood, other kids always wanted to take over. But we wanted control of the neighborhood around our home. We made some friends with some kids on our street. Eventually, we kicked a lot of the people out. It was our yard, so they really had no business being there anyway. Besides, we would get into street fights only because we were new on the block. My brothers and I would go to the elementary school, and guys would challenge us. "Oh, you're from L.A., huh?" A lot of guys just wanted to test you out. So, we would fight.

Everybody would show up at our house for parties. Relatives came from Mexico, and my father's compadres (friends), all came to the house. On the weekends, there was a large menu of offerings: menudo, pozole, you name it. Everybody would bring food for the potlucks. At one point, the men began gambling. First it was penny ante, you know, just pennies and nickels. Over time, it got to a point where a lot of people were losing their paychecks. It got kind of ugly. We didn't even know some of the people who were playing there. It wasn't just relatives anymore. It was like the word got out, "Hey, there's a card game at the Rodriguez house." And all kinds of strangers would show up.

Finally, my mom told my dad, "You know, some of the guys were cheating, bending the cards and marking the cards."

My dad agreed. "No more. Somebody is gonna end up being killed." He didn't want any problems from the neighborhood or the police, so he stopped the gambling.

My mom and dad, when they were alone, they could speak English well enough to get by. But if one of us were with them they'd look at us and ask in Spanish, "What did they say? Tell them this, tell them that." We were their interpreters. During the school year, they would sacrifice to make sure we had clothes and things for school. Now it was up to us to turn around and translate for them. But I have seen my dad when he got pissed off when he was misunderstood or ignored by clerks. Man, some of the words that came out of his mouth were unbelievable. But most of the time he got along with people.

We had found out that they were going to start a Teen Post at the old fire station in South El Monte. Some home boys, you know, typical cholos and veteranos from the community, had gotten access to the building from the city government. Some people called it a teen center, it was considered a City Parks and Recreation program. But everyone knew it as a Teen Post. After a short time, the old fire station had a pool table, a ping pong table, and large open spaces inside. In the back, they also had a basketball court. It had transformed from a fire department into a youth center.

THE BIRTH OF A WARRIOR

We found out that they were teaching boxing. So, everybody from our neighborhood said, "Wow, let's go learn how to box, man. They have a boxing coach over there." We were already into boxing—or should I say street fighting. We went over there to check it out. Three guys were running it, and they brought a box out. Inside the box were nothing but gloves. Boxing gloves, big old walrus gloves. They were actually training gloves.

They lined us up, smallest to the biggest, it didn't matter the age, and put gloves on us. And they said, "Okay, you two first," pointing at some kids, and they would start fighting. Then it was the next two kids' turn to fight. We'd get the gloves from the other guys. When it was my turn, I put the gloves on against one of the guys from the neighborhood. We started swinging at each other with no instructions, no nothing. It was puro chingasos (just fucking fighting)!

I turned around and I looked at the instructors. They were cracking up laughing at us. They were having a ball watching us beat the shit out of each other. These instructors were supposed to be training us. Instead, they were getting high and having a couple of beers and talking amongst themselves. They weren't teaching us anything! So, I got pissed. I took off the gloves and I threw the gloves at them. Fortunately, my aim was good, I hit one of the trainers in the face. He chased after me, but I was too quick and got away. That was my introduction to boxing. But that opportunity had disappeared as quickly as it had begun.

Not long after that, I found out that they were teaching karate there. I didn't know what karate was, and my friends were all clamoring, "Hey, there are some guys at the Teen Post in pajamas, and they're doing Chinese fighting or something." Bruce Lee, the martial artist, had just started acting as the character

Kato from the *Green Hornet* television series. It seemed everybody was talking about karate.

I was in junior high and was bored, just hanging out, so I said, "Hey, let's go check it out." Well, I recall vividly, seeing all these people come into the Teen Post wearing what looked like robes. The instructors put students in different rooms. In one room, they had the little kids, and in another they had the teenagers and adult beginners. And they did this funny thing to begin the practice.

They spread their legs and bent their knees down, like they were on a horse and moved their arms in circular motions from one side to the other. Then they pushed a leg out and continued to move their arms up and down. They looked like slow dancers. I thought to myself, *This is a little sissy thing! Maricones.* That was my thought; *This isn't like boxing, this isn't real Chingasos.*

But when they started fighting, they began doing different movements and stuff I'd never seen before. They started what looked like a dance step, and everybody copied the same moves. At that point it started getting a little bit better, especially when they started sparring. It was fast and furious, boom, boom, boom! Wow, especially when the adults were fighting. Man, I was impressed. They started doing all kinds of kicks, elbows, knees, and punches that looked like they were coming from everywhere. They called it LimaLama, and I wanted to learn it! Eventually, my brother Hector, my sister Leticia, and my younger brother Ruben all trained in LimaLama.

TRAINING UNDER MASTER SAL

The year was 1968 and I was 13 years old and wanted to learn LimaLama. The LimaLama master was Salomon "Sal" Esquivel, who was one of the five original black belt Masters under Grandmaster (GM) Tu'umanmao "Tino" Tuiolosega. Master Sal had a large group of students learning LimaLama at the

THE BIRTH OF A WARRIOR

teen center. It cost a dollar a lesson, and I couldn't afford it. My Uncle Manuel decided to join too, and he paid for my brother and me to have lessons. If you brought someone in, then you didn't have to pay.

My Uncle Tito was always ready to have a good time. He was an adventurer. He'd have everyone chip in for gas, and he would drive until we were lost, just to find new places. He would take us fishing and camping. So why not try martial arts too? But he didn't stay long before he quit.

Sal was teaching the students but also had other black belts assisting him. I didn't know it then, but I was about to learn a new martial art form, created in Los Angeles in the early 1960's, that was practically unknown among the legendary fighting systems of judo, kung fu, muay Thai, jiu-jitsu, taekwondo, and karate.

On the first day, the black belts put all the new trainees in a separate room to learn basic punches and strengthening exercises. We were told to take the horse position, legs shoulder width apart, in a half squat. Our instructor, I would learn later, was Master Sal's oldest son, Sal Jr. Sal Jr. decided to show us how to "K-yae" and take a punch to the mid-section. First, he hit my uncle, who was knocked back from his horse position. Then Sal Jr. hit my brother Hector, knocking the wind out of him as he hit the floor.

When he came to me, I just thought to myself, *Fuck that. He's not going to hit me.* And when he tried to hit me, I punched him in the face. We immediately started fighting, and the commotion brought Master Sal and others into the room, who quickly separated us. Master Sal believed Sal Jr.'s version of what had just transpired. I think they viewed me as just a little thug, so they threw me out of training. My uncle and brother had no choice but to leave with me, because I had no ride home. Before

I ever had a martial arts lesson, I had already been expelled for fighting with the martial arts instructor.

I was embarrassed and angry but still wanted to learn LimaLama. I didn't have the dollar to pay, so I decided I would attend the practices anyway with my uncle and brother and sit and watch them train. I would try to mimic the moves the students made, trying hard to remember everything without anyone noticing.

One of the LimaLama instructors was "Humbos." He was a black guy who had seen me sitting every day just watching the training. I would try to memorize the techniques and then go home and practice them. Humbos must have taken a liking to me. One day, he called me over after class and taught me a fighting combination. He would make me repeat it and repeat it, over and over again, until I got it right. Then, I would go home and practice, practice, practice. He had shown me hitting combinations with full or half drag kicks.

Humbos was teaching me these fighting combinations on the sly. Master Sal was not aware of it. The next time, I would come back and watch the whole class, absorbing like a sponge anything new being shown to the students. After class, I would show Humbos my combinations. I wanted to prove to him that I had been practicing. The problem was, he had been showing me only attacking moves. I didn't know there were also moves to counter strikes. I had been doing this secret training for about three months.

Me being me, I would pick fights at Kranz Junior High. I would pick fights just to see if my LimaLama lessons actually worked. I wasn't angry or mean about it; I was curious to see if LimaLama was for real in a real fight. I still got hit, because a lot of those guys were bigger than me, but, you know, I would try it out. I must have had at least one fight every month from junior high to high school. All I knew at the time was attack,

THE BIRTH OF A WARRIOR

attack, attack. And the LimaLama lessons seemed to work. I never tried to hurt anyone, I only meant to beat on them till they gave up. I really gained a lot of confidence in myself as a fighter.

Everyone knew who the toughest guys in school were. Those guys ended up in more fights because there was always someone looking to challenge them. One of my neighbors, Richard Moreno, was a tough guy in our neighborhood. He always got into fights and beat up a lot of guys. Everyone knew not to mess around with him. He was the guy to beat.

We used to hang out together. One day, we decided to ditch school and go to Legg Lake. The lake was about two miles from my house. When we got there, we decided to swim to a small island in the middle of the lake. We were almost to the island, but Richard couldn't make it, he was drowning. I had to grab him by his hair and pull him to the island. I ended up having to swim back to shore to find a paddle boat to bring him back. He was really embarrassed.

When we got back to his house, I started clowning him about being a pussy for not being able to make it to the island. He didn't like it and got angry. I told him, "The reason I don't fight you in school is because I don't want anyone to know I can fight. But here in your backyard, I'm going to kick your ass." We ended up fighting, and I beat him up. Afterwards I told him, "Just between you and me, you know who the best is now. Remember, I don't want the reputation of being the toughest guy in school. I don't want all these idiots coming after me. I don't need to fight for no good reason."

I still considered him a friend, acknowledging him at school or in the neighborhood, but we went our separate ways after that fight. Nobody ever knew I had beaten him up. And he got to keep his reputation as a tough guy in school. I had started hanging out with a different crowd. I went deeper into martial arts and started working summers with the City Parks and Recreation. Richard, unfortunately, started hanging out with cholos and got caught up in that lifestyle.

MY FIRST TOURNAMENT

Master Sal's LimaLama school was getting ready for a karate tournament, so I decided I was going too. I wasn't a student in his school, and I had no karate gi. I didn't even have the money to sign up. But I convinced my Uncle Manuel to take me to the tournament. He bought my white uniform gi for 10 bucks, if that much, and the entrance fee. I didn't know how to tie the white belt and just put it in a knot. I ended up using a piece of cardboard for a mouthpiece. I folded it up, with the white color showing, and I put it in my mouth. For a cup, I borrowed one from a guy at the school—and just stuck the dirty thing in my underwear.

I fought. I didn't know what the hell I was doing. I just did whatever Humbos had taught me, plus my instincts from street fighting. The only thing the judges told me was, "No hits to the face; they are illegal and if you draw blood, you will be disqualified." So, without any reservations, I went for it! I made it all the way to the semi-finals.

I began to get attention from the crowd during my fights. I guess the people in attendance could see I wasn't trying to score points; I was just fighting. My opponents were trying to score points, but I was trying to hurt them—kicks to the groin, body shots to the ribs. I just fought as hard and fast as I could. One of the LimaLama students, Danny Esquivel, noticed me. Danny was the son of Master Sal.

He knew that to participate in the tournament, you had to belong to a recognized school, but I didn't belong to any school officially. I wasn't training with the LimaLama school. I wasn't paying the dollar a class. So, Danny told the main referee, "Hey,

THE BIRTH OF A WARRIOR

man, that guy don't belong to no school." The referee realized I had no martial arts patch and I was wearing a brand-new uniform. They decided to disqualify me as I stood on the mat ready for my next fight, which was the semi-final. They wouldn't let me fight anymore.

I realized I was in real trouble. Suddenly, everybody started clapping and chanting, "Hey, let him fight, let him fight, let him fight."

Danny told his dad, Master Sal, "Look, Lorenzo is fighting, but he's not representing us. But he already made the finals." I think Danny convinced his father to let me continue to fight.

Master Sal spoke with the tournament referees: "He already made the finals, so let him fight." The referees agreed and allowed me to continue.

So, I fought as an independent. And I had the crowd following. I was one of the four remaining fighters. If I won the first match, then I would fight for first or second place. If I lost, then I would be fighting for third or fourth. I was ready and excited. As soon as the referee said "Go," Bam, bam, bam, I attacked my opponent just like Humbos taught me, and, without realizing it, I instinctively punched the guy in the face. The poor guy started bleeding, and the referee separated us, and he disqualified me. I was looking around. "What did I do wrong? It's a fight!"

The referee shook his head in disagreement. "No, no, no, you can't hit the face." So, then all I could do now was to compete for third place. This time, I really tried not to hit my opponent in the face, but the guy kept sticking his face out, almost inviting me to hit it. *Bam, bam, boom,* I kicked him right in the face and I got disqualified again. You don't get a trophy for fourth place. So, I guess I had won the battles but lost the war.

After the tournament, Master Sal pulled me aside and chewed me out. "You have to represent a school, and you have to have permission. The only reason I let you fight was because all these people were rooting for you, and you had already made the final round." He was right. And I was wrong. But I was proud of myself. The following day, I was a little bruised and sore, but really happy. I had survived. I sometimes wondered how my opponents must have felt after I had been pounding their bodies.

Most of the time, when I got into a street fight, I never got hurt but I'd get in trouble. I recall some neighborhood kids who lived about three houses away from us. They sent the youngest of their brothers after my little brother just to make him cry. They were bullies. I would go after the little kid for hitting my brother. Then, they'd come after me, thinking they were going to kick my ass. I ended up fighting one brother, then the next brother, until I got to the oldest one.

Like a family tree, I would knock all those family limbs down. But their mom would tell my mom that I kicked her son's butt. So, my mom would give me a spanking and then my dad would get home and give me another one. The next day I would start again with those guys because they had gotten me in trouble at home. It was a never-ending story.

The thing about competing in my first martial arts tournament? This kind of fighting was different. I made it to the finals and got fourth place, not bad. I told myself, *Hey, I'm not going to get in trouble with my parents for fighting in tournaments.* Besides, I appreciated all these strangers applauding and patting me on the back and saying, "You know, you got something there boy…" and "You did good, young man." That was a lot of attention for a young man my age, and it was from people I didn't even know. I was just fighting instinctively. I was a beginner, and I knew I could be better. It was not that I was trying to hurt anybody. Okay, maybe I was, but I was doing something I liked to do—fight—and it felt good winning. I wanted more.

CHIQUITO PERO PICOSO

My dad had a heavy hand. After I had started serious training in LimaLama, I recall he'd put his hand on my shoulder and give me this look like he was gonna hit me. I'd say, "Hey dad, be nice!"

He'd respond, "Hey, you get up in the ring and they hit you, right?"

I'd look at him, not sure what he was intending to do, and say, "Yeah, but I can hit back."

Without changing his expression, he'd say, "You can hit me back, but I hit too! I brought you into this world, and I'll take you out." That was his thing, always reminding us subtly and sometimes not so subtly, who was in charge of the house.

Now, I've seen my older brother Hector fight. I recall seeing him hit a guy and it was over. He knocked him out. Hector also trained in LimaLama and had earned his brown belt while in high school. But I think he stopped training because he broke some guy's ribs. He didn't want to hurt anybody. Me, I was the opposite. Put somebody in front of me, and you knew it was over. You shouldn't have put him in front of me because I had bad intentions. I wanted to hurt them. By the time we had moved to South El Monte, I had already gotten into plenty of fights. I'm the tallest one in my family, and I'm short. I'm five foot six. I used to call Hector my "little big brother" because he was shorter than me.

Later, as an adult, I'd share stories of my fights with some of my students. Most of them weighed two hundred plus pounds, and all were taller than me. Joking, they would step up close and look down at me saying, "Hey, shorty."

I'd respond, "That's right. But this shorty can still kick your ass!" And they knew it, as they'd quickly back away. They knew I wasn't kidding.

A dollar a lesson. That is what it cost to train in LimaLama. That was a lot of money in those days. I received an allowance each week for lunch or the bus, and I used that to pay for my lessons. I wanted to go five days a week. If I brought someone with me, I could train for free. We would train Mondays and Wednesdays. We were learning all the basics in fighting, punches, combinations, and kicks. There were no punching bags to practice on; we were the punching bags. We always got hit when we sparred. One thing that Master Sal and Grandmaster Tino were fond of saying to us: "You gotta feel it, to learn it. LimaLama doesn't back up." That was their constant mantra for sparring. Make contact like you mean it.

There weren't any mats or mirrors either. The Teen Post was actually an empty building where the fire trucks were parked. So, we practiced on the cement floor. Later, when the Teen Post was closed, we moved to Master Sal's garage, which was also located in South El Monte. In fact, all my training as a youth was on cement or outdoor pavement. I was never trained in a real martial arts school. All our training took place at church parking lots or parks-and-recreation gyms, tennis courts, or basketball courts. I had no idea what a real dojo or martial arts studio looked like.

The first time I entered a martial arts studio, I saw all these fancy emblems, and framed pictures of revered martial arts masters. More importantly, the studios had mats, mirrors, and fighting equipment for the hands, feet, and head. These studios looked too pretty to be used for real fighting. The mats felt like pillows under my feet. As much as I wanted to get knocked down to feel the cushy mats, that wasn't going to happen. Those dojo students would need those pillowed floor mats to cushion their fall after we were through knocking them to the ground.

THE BIRTH OF A WARRIOR

Master Sal had a lot of dedicated students who stayed with him when we moved to his garage to train. We had some of our best fights there over the years. A lot of famous fighters in martial arts would go there to learn or polish their fighting skills. Full-contact fighting had just started. I didn't know much about the details, but I was excited because we could go full blast when fighting. Like our training, no pulling shots. I got to witness our brown and black belts fighting these famous martial artists. None wore protective head or hand equipment. It was spooky. These visitors wanted to fight but didn't want other people to see them fight, especially if they lost. It was common to see a couple of knockouts each night. Everyone there wanted to be the best. Master Sal's fighters were too tough, and many of those visitors never came back.

Jim Kelly, of the movie *Into the Dragon* fame, was a master of Shōrin-Ryū Karate. He would attend Master Sal's LimaLama garage school training. Not long after, he went on to win the World Middleweight title in 1971 at the Long Beach International Karate Championships. It was a testament to the respect LimaLama garnered among elite martial artists and Master Sal's training regime. I recall when Master Sal promoted a tournament at El Monte High School. Kelly showed up in a brand new 240Z, his huge afro on his six-foot, one-inch frame, stepping out of that sports car. I loved it. I wanted to be like him, and I wanted the car even more!

I had quite a bit of fights during my early training days. Some fights, I started just to test my skills. But any fight I got into, I made sure to finish. Most of my friends were all bigger than me, and whenever we went someplace, people always seemed to pick on the smallest guy. I was that guy. But I never backed down from anybody. Yeah, I used to say, "Chiquito, pero picoso!" (Small, but fiery!)

I recall one fight that occurred on the handball court at El Monte High School. I was a freshman at the time. This guy and I were playing handball for money. Everyone who played handball in El Monte played for money. He belonged to one of the local street gangs, and there were plenty of them—Flores, Hicks, Hayes, White Fence, and Mariana, but most belonged to Monte Flores. I never belonged to a gang, but I lived in a barrio full of gang members.

I had just beaten the dude in handball, but he decided not to pay me because, he claimed, he had no money. I told him, "Hey if I lost, I would've paid you. Why are you betting when you have no money?"

He flipped me off saying, "Fuck you, I ain't paying you."

He was disrespectful. Anytime you bet, you have to pay up. For Mexicans, if your word is no good, you're not shit. That was the bottom line. I told him, "I'm going to kick your ass if you don't give me the money. I don't care where you get it from. Get it from your brother, your mother or friends—I don't give a fuck. Let's go to your car or locker, wherever."

He didn't say a word because he didn't give a shit. He stepped back into a fighting stance. So, I moved forward and hit him. I punched him right in the face. As he was going down, I kicked him in the groin. When he hit the pavement, I jumped on him and hit him three more times to the face. I was only a blue belt, but I had plenty of practice hitting people. He was trying to fight back. But then I saw a shadow coming at me from the periphery. Two of his friends were running over and trying to jump into the fray. It seems anytime gangbangers were in a group, they were brave. Only when they were alone, could you tell if they had any heart.

These guys had some heart. They just didn't know how to fight. When the first guy tried to kick me, I grabbed his leg pulling toward me using his momentum to drop him to the

THE BIRTH OF A WARRIOR

ground. I immediately stood up and kicked him. I grabbed the second guy by the hair and spun around him, using him as a shield. The handball guy was still on the ground and didn't want to get up. The first guy had jumped off the pavement and was swinging wild, trying to hit me. But he could only hit my human shield. I tossed my human shield to the ground and hit the first guy in the face. I swept his leg, tripping him to the ground, and kicked him in the head. During the fight, I mostly got hit in the back of the head and shoulders.

When the fight started, my friends had seen the commotion, and they wanted to see what I would do, which pissed me off. They really didn't want to jump in until they knew the fight was almost over or if I was losing. It didn't matter; I was used to fighting alone. Besides, most of my friends were also my students in LimaLama. They knew if they got into trouble, I had their back. I never considered needing someone to have my back. But, if they saw me outnumbered, they should have at least come over to even the odds. That was the difference between me and most guys I knew; I had no fear of being outnumbered.

THE CLELAND HOUSE

I was about 16 when Master Sal changed our gi colors from white to black. I couldn't afford to buy a black uniform, so my sister dyed it black for me. By that time, Master Sal had moved us to East Los Angeles at the Cleland House, a United Way funded non-profit organization that catered to the neighborhood in East Los Angeles. Its mission was a noble but difficult task: to get youth off the streets and into programs. It had a pool, large meeting rooms, and one area large enough for practicing dance or, in our case, martial arts. A lot of cholos and wannabe gangbangers hung out at the Cleland House. It was located on Dozier Street between City Terrace, East Los

Angeles, and Monterey Park, the mecca of gangs in southern California.

When new people, especially young people showed up, the cholos would always ask, "De donde?" (Where are you from?) They wanted to know what clicka (gang) we belonged to.

We'd try to tell them, "We're from nowhere, we just came to train." But they'd go on and on with the questions, challenging us, so we had to fight.

One time, this cholo actually came into the room as we were training. In those days, he was probably high on pills or paint thinner. He tried choosing a fight with anyone, yelling, "You guys ain't shit. Who's the toughest motherfucker here?"

Master Sal motioned to one of the brown belt instructors, "Hey, go take care of that guy." So, the instructor walked over to the cholo, telling the guy to leave, but the cholo pulled out a big knife. I remember watching and thinking to myself, *Damn, this is gonna be fun to watch.* We had been learning some knife techniques, and I wasn't yet comfortable with training in weapons. I wanted to see what was going to happen. It never occurred to me that the situation had just turned dangerous.

Master Sal wasn't taking any more of the interruption. He immediately walked over and told the guy to leave. The cholo ignored him and squared off for a knife fight. Master Sal calmy told him, "If you don't get out of here, you're gonna be wearing that knife." The cholo kept talking shit and suddenly swung the knife at Master Sal. Master Sal blocked the homie's knife attack, striking his forearm and in the same motion he hit the cholo repeatedly, boom, boom, boom. Before the cholo hit the ground, he was unconscious.

Master Sal had put a big cut on his head and broken his jaw, some ribs, and his arm. He had to be taken by ambulance to the hospital. I heard that the cholo sued Master Sal for his injuries. It wasn't the first time Master Sal had been in trouble because

THE BIRTH OF A WARRIOR

of his martial arts skills. When he got into a fight, he fully intended to hurt someone badly.

After that incident, we were always prepared to fight when we arrived at the Cleland House. Because they wanted to get back at us, the cholos burned the car top of one of our guys' convertible car. If we had to use the restroom, three or four guys would follow us inside and we'd have to fight our way out. I remember having to pee and when I turned around some guy would block the door. I'd tell him, "Let us out."

The cholo would say, "No. Give us your money." So, we would fight our way out. It happened so often that, after a while, Master Sal made us go to the restroom two or three at a time for protection. The same with the girls who trained in LimaLama.

Other martial arts gyms would be invited by Master Sal to train with us. Because there were no trophies or rewards, it was just fighting for pride. My instinct was, *You came to my house. You're not gonna kick my ass in my house.* These matches were always better than fighting in the tournaments. We were fighting hard core because it was for our honor as LimaLama fighters. We fought mostly Japanese karate and some kung fu gyms. They were too fancy with their kicks. We'd eat them alive. It didn't take long for them to turn down invitations. They didn't want to be beat down anymore.

As I progressed in my training, I wanted to test myself. But not in my neighborhood or school, where I could get in trouble with my parents or the local gangs. Instead, I would go to the beach and challenge the Navy *Squid* and Marine *Jarhead* recruits who were drinking and hanging out at the piers while on leave. I'd invite some friends to go but wouldn't share my intentions with them. But I knew they'd have my back if something bad happened. I didn't have anything against the military, and I wasn't an angry or frustrated young man. I just wanted to know if my training in LimaLama really worked in a fight. I just thought it was best to test myself with strangers outside of my neighborhood.

I would walk on the pier until I made eye contact with some *Squid or Jarhead* I saw. They were easy to spot in dorky clothes and cropped haircuts. I'd call them out for making eye contact with me, cursing, anything to start a fight. There was always one guy who took the bait. They'd charge at me and the fight was on. Some of them would get their licks in, catching me in the head or body, but I'd always win the fight. Even better, when one or two of their buddies would jump in to help, I'd kick their asses too. It was better than tournament fights because there were no rules or minute rounds. You just threw chingasos (blows) until someone quit or got hurt.

It was fun, and I never got in trouble with the law because guys in the military didn't want to risk getting caught fighting with civilians. They were willing to give as good as they got. I appreciated those fights. For me they were just juvenile delinquent "dust-ups." I made sure not to injure anyone. Just toe-to-toe fighting, with no serious injuries sustained by anyone, but plenty of bumps and bruises to make their weekend complete.

Thinking back about it now, I realize it was stupid and dangerous. Someone could have been seriously hurt, including me. But I was so fixated on being the best fighter I could be, I just craved real-life conflicts to see if my training was effective. I didn't drink or use drugs as a youth, but I readily admit I was addicted to fighting.

We had all the gangs from the area at our school. I wasn't in a gang, but everyone wanted me to join because they knew I could fight. So, you had to pay attention to all the cliques. Lomas, White Fence, Varrio Nuevo, Monte Flores, Hicks, Hayes, etc. When I went to school, my clothes and shoes were always hand-me-downs from my brother: Pendleton's, Dickies, or Levi's. Those were all our parents would buy. They were cheap

THE BIRTH OF A WARRIOR

and they would last a long time. I never followed clothing trends because I couldn't afford it. All my money was for martial arts or the occasional date with a girl.

I remember this guy, "Apache," a Mexican with long hair. He was a few years older than me. Bell bottom pants had just come out, and he cut his Levi's pants at the bottom and added material to turn them into bell bottoms. Everyone thought he was cool. All the girls wanted to be with him. This guy could also fight. I had seen him fight in junior high; man, that guy got down! He dominated guys during a fight because they weren't speedy enough to beat him. I remember we'd play touch football, and no one could catch him; he was like a cat, too quick and agile. By the time we all got to high school, a lot of guys would challenge him to fight. You know, young guys trying to see who the new rooster would be in the crowd. He was just too fast and strong for anyone else to handle.

During my high school years, I always started the school year looking to start a fight. I'd pick the biggest guy in my physical education class and challenge him by making up some lie to piss him off. P.E. class was the best place for this encounter. Everyone would be on the field or volleyball court to witness it. My intended victim would come at me, and I'd hit him fast and hard, knocking him down. If he thought about getting up, I'd finish him off, but never enough to injure him physically.

I figured if I got my ass beat, who cares? People would think he's a bully. I did get hit a few times in these fights but never got my ass kicked. It was a challenge for me, but I admit I instigated the whole thing. When the school vice principal investigated, I'd say the dude had been picking on me all summer and I couldn't take it anymore. Of course, I was a little guy, and had purposely chosen a victim who was twice my size, so they'd believe me. School officials always let me go with only a stern warning. The word would get around that I was either crazy or a firecracker when I got mad. I didn't care what anyone said about me. My plan worked: no one bothered me at school the rest of the year. And my parents never found out about it.

GRANDMASTER TINO

The first time I saw Grandmaster (GM) Tino Tuiolosega was at the Cleland House. He looked like a giant to me. I was maybe 14 years old. He was a six-foot, two-inch tall mountain of a man. There was a hush from everyone in the room as he entered. Everyone moved out of his way as he walked to the mats. He shook hands with all of us youngsters. His hand devoured mine. That was the first time I noticed that all the adults seemed in awe of him or feared him. But everyone gave him respect as the grandmaster. I had never seen grown men with fear in their eyes until then. Later, when I returned from military service, I would be fortunate to study directly under GM Tino. Only then did I realize why he was so intimidating. He had bad intentions when he hit you, and that included sparring practice, where he expected you to strike hard and be hit hard. And when you didn't try to hit him, he'd hit you harder!

Master Al Garza told the story about the Original Five black belts under GM Tino in his book, *My Story; Memories of a Martial Art Grandmaster*. The five masters had been learning the newly created LimaLama techniques from him. One day, GM Tino mentioned the power of the Dim Mok. They laughed, challenging his knowledge of the Dim Mok, the so-called "death touch" strike (Drop punch/Finger Set technique). Master Garza identified the five original students as having been fierce martial arts competitors before beginning their tutelage under GM Tino. But, in training or tournaments, GM Tino had known no equal.

GM Tino had never shown any of his students the Dim Mok, and so they smirked and teased him, saying, "Yeah, right, the death strike." GM Tino became incensed by their disrespect and

THE BIRTH OF A WARRIOR

ordered each of them to attack him. Master Garza described how Master Tiny, Sal, and John took their best shots at attacking GM Tino. None of them could describe what had happened next, as they lay on the floor in excruciating pain. They never saw the punch that struck them down. The strike was too fast and inflicted large bruising injuries that took weeks to heal. None of them ever doubted GM Tino again.

Master Garza witnessed the bruising on Master Sal from the strike. He related that GM Tino was friends with Bruce Lee, who visited him frequently when he was in southern California during the mid-1960s. They both also spent time with GM Ed Parker at his karate studio. Master Garza asked GM Tino if the Dim Mok punch was similar to Bruce Lee's one-inch punch. GM Tino responded, "Bruce Lee's punch is more like a push. Mine is a strike."

This story stuck with me years later when I studied under GM Tino. I wasn't about to question or joke about anything he said. I wouldn't do that with Master Sal either. I had too much respect for their martial arts abilities and a constant awareness of their short tempers. Unfortunately, I had the same ignorance that Sal had when he trained under GM Tino. I always tested Master Sal when he demonstrated strike techniques. I'd be the first to say, "Hey, show me." And Master Sal would proceed to put a serious hurt on my body. Later on, as I got older, I got smarter. I'd say, "Show me!" and I'd put the biggest guy I could find in front of him. By then I was saying, "No, no, no. I'm small compared to you, so you can do whatever you want. Do it to this guy, then I know that it works."

Sal was the same when he trained with GM Tino, in that, he always wanted to test and feel it. Sal repeated GM Tino's favorite saying: "You gotta feel it to learn it." The rest of us were all willing and able test dummies, looking to hit something or get hit.

I never challenged Master Sal; I had too much respect for him. But I always tried to beat him when we sparred. It never ended well; I got beat up every time. I didn't care because I wanted to learn. As I progressed in training and made the brown belt level, I finally realized that Master Sal fought differently, in tournaments or visitor demonstrations, from how he was training us. We always trained in a wide stance. Yet, his stance was smaller.

I would watch him every chance I got. First, his attitude would change; he was uncharacteristically focused. I noticed he'd get in a "T" stance, something akin to a Wing Chung or Ba Gua figure-eight stance, and then he'd put his arms in an abbreviated "T" shape. You couldn't get into it. He would always move forward, eventually wearing you out. If he were in a ring, you were in trouble, because he'd ultimately corner you and then you were finished. He was too quick and deadly with his strikes. This is what I wanted to do too. I was always focused and ready to fight in any tournament I ever entered. I treated every tournament opponent like it was a street fight or bar fight: I was determined to kick my challenger's ass. I wanted to be like Sal and Tino.

TOURNAMENT FIGHTS

I had competed in hundreds of local tournaments before the age of 18. In those days, maybe more so than today, your reputation was on the line. In tournaments, you had to earn it. If you lost to a nobody, someone who had never won a tournament, then your reputation was damaged. I made sure that never happened. There were some guys who purposely stuck their head out during a tournament fight to get hit. They'd get hit and bite their lip to draw blood and say they got hit. Then I would be disqualified for hitting the face. I remember I kicked this guy so hard, I lifted him off the canvas. He ran around the

THE BIRTH OF A WARRIOR

ring so much, I had to chase him to hit him. When I kicked him, I didn't control the kick and he went up in the air. He was hurting so bad, they had to take him out on a stretcher to the hospital. I had earned the reputation of being a tough fighter. I didn't go to tournaments to score points, and everyone knew it. I went to fight.

Of all the tournaments I fought in by the time I was 18, I only lost two. I lost because I was disqualified for hitting the face or the groin. I had won the fights but lost the war. I know I would have gladly competed in larger tournaments if I had had the money. But I didn't have the means to go to the big tournaments. I remember there was a national tournament in Las Vegas. It was early 1973. But we had to pay for the room, gas, and meals. And we wanted to party too!

It cost money to attend a big tournament. All that money just for a $20.00 trophy. And if we got hurt, there was no insurance for a hospital visit. If I was lucky enough to go to a big tournament, I wasn't thinking about the consequences, I only cared about fighting and winning. I recall a big tournament that Danny Esquivel and I entered. We did good. Danny won the black belt Lightweight division, and I won the brown belt Lightweight division.

Daniel, as a black belt, was already rated nationally. I had fought black belts regularly in sparring, and in some tournaments. But I hadn't tested yet as a black belt, so I had no rating assigned to me. I recall when I would take Danny to the airport to compete out of state or for an international tournament. I was so envious. I told myself, *I want to be the guy someday, who travels the world to fight.*

I recall fighting in a huge tournament in Culver City. I was maybe 16 or 17. I was with Danny, who was fighting in the black belt Lightweight division. I was fighting in the brown belt Lightweight division. There was a long line for signups, and as it got shorter and shorter, I saw this guy standing by the table. I found out later that he was from New York. By the time it was my turn to sign-in, I was standing right next to him. He asked me, "Aren't you going to leave?"

I said, "Why?"

"Don't you know who I am?"

I looked at him sarcastically. "Oh, you're somebody?"

"Yeah, I just won the Battle of Atlanta."

I responded, "Good, so that means, when I beat you, I beat somebody!"

"Oh, you think you're going to win. You think I flew all the way from Atlanta to come to California to lose?"

I just looked at him. He was a little bigger than me, but most of my opponents were bigger than me. We were both in the Lightweight division. We ended up fighting in the 2nd or 3rd round, and I beat him!

He was actually a damn good fighter. But I never gave him a chance because he had already told me he had won a major tournament. I wasn't going to allow him to get an advantage. I was determined to kick his ass. As soon as the referee said, "Go," *Boom!* I was right on top of him. I just beat him up. After the tournament, he came to me and said, "We should have fought for the Grand Champion at the end. Who are you?"

I looked at him and said, "You know, I'm the one that just beat the guy from the Battle of Atlanta." I did tell him my name and, of course, my reputation was now known in the state of Georgia. I won the Lightweight Division Championship that day but lost on points in the Grand Championship fight.

THE BULL RING

Curtis Faust was a black belt who came from one of the southern states. Arkansas, I think. He wore a satin gung fu gi. Everybody was talking about him. Master Sal had given him my

THE BIRTH OF A WARRIOR

classes to teach when I was working the youth camp during the summer. I thought, *Why is he teaching my class? He can't teach it because he doesn't know LimaLama.* We ended up fighting in the torture circle, what we later renamed the bull ring.

Sal would routinely set up the bull ring so that his students would have to fight guys that he wanted you to fight. He had all his students make a large circle. Fighters had to remain inside the circle and fight whoever was picked by Master Sal. He'd make you fight every guy in the circle just to wear you out. But I wanted it. It was good for stamina building and kept you sharp in technique. He always saved the strongest opponent for you to fight last. It was frustrating because I always wanted the best guy first. I preferred fighting the best guy when I was fresh and alert. But that was Sal's way of taking away your advantage and teaching you to focus or get hit. He made you earn your wins.

He put Curtis against me last. Curtis was a grown man, and I was still in high school. It didn't matter, we went toe to toe. The whole school was watching. Sal wanted Curtis to know that he was only fighting a brown belt and Curtis still had more to learn to be an accomplished black belt in LimaLama. Curtis was really good. Master Sal also wanted to test me to see if I had slacked off my training while I was working the summer youth camp.

At the time, all of us were training for an international tournament sponsored by Grandmaster Ed Parker. Later I learned that Curtis had already won one of the internationals and was a ranked karate fighter. At that time, Danny Esquivel, Master Sal's son, was rated as a "top six" fighter for California. I didn't know anything about the rankings and didn't care. All I needed to know was, *Can you kick my ass? If you can kick my ass, I'll respect your ranking.* Curtis never did kick my ass. But we did kick each other's ass. He was tough.

Years later, I learned that GM Tino was not happy with Curtis. Curtis had started training with GM Tino, then went to Sal. He did this twice. Tino was not happy with that behavior. There is an element of trust and respect that Curtis may have failed to understand. It was unspoken but something I would later understand when I tried to train in different martial art schools in South Korea. If you are good, then you should devote yourself completely to your chosen martial art style. You can always incorporate other style forms or techniques to strengthen your own style, but always honoring your original style. I tried to honor my LimaLama roots and be humble when observing or learning a new style. However, a few times in South Korea, I was forced to leave my humble demeanor at the door.

We started teaching at the Barrio Boxing Center in 1971. There weren't a lot of boxers, and Master Sal had us signing up people who were going to train in boxing. But we were training them all in LimaLama. The place came with a boxing ring and all the equipment. The manager got paid for running the program, and Master Sal had a place to teach and train. It was a win-win for everyone. Eventually, I ended up teaching there. I kinda took over the program.

At the beginning of class, everyone would pay their dollar. There were three separate classes with sixty or more people every Wednesday and Friday. I'd collect the monies and deliver them to Master Sal at the end of the day. In return, I would be able to train and assist him in his private classes. There was a lot of sparring and fighting in those sessions. I recall a couple of years before I had tested for my blue belt, I ended up fighting Master Richard Nuñez's son, who was testing for his black belt. We had a really good fight, but I whipped his ass. Master Sal was there when it happened. I don't think Master Richard ever forgave me for whipping his son.

THE BIRTH OF A WARRIOR

Master Sal and Master Richard competed in everything. Master Richard's son would compete in the Katas (Forms) competition. But when he'd fight, he would drop down to the brown belt. I'm not sure why; it made no sense to me in terms of competition. Why wouldn't he want to fight the best black belts? I didn't care for Kata competition, because it wasn't fighting. It simulates actual fighting because it allows the practitioner to feel and experience the coordinated movements at full speed and full power without having to "pull" the technique as you would do with a training partner. But the way Master Sal and Master Richard taught us, there was no pulling punches. You hit or get hit!

I viewed Katas as a dancing form. Master Sal made me compete in Katas because he wanted me to have the experience. I did well, I placed in those competitions. But I suspect he also wanted someone to compete against Master Richard's son. I was a brown belt at the time and purposely stood next to Master Richard's son at the tournaments. Many times, he would go to the heavyweight division, but not to fight.

When I showed up at tournaments, I would try to find out who was more recognized by other competitors, who was ranked or had a reputation. Sometimes, the officials wouldn't let me fight in the heavyweight division because I didn't make the weight requirement, so I had no choice but to fight as a lightweight. Once I won the lightweight, I'd jump to the welterweight, middleweight, or heavyweight. But if the tournament had a Grand Champion trophy, the winners of the four divisions were allowed to fight each other for the title. I looked forward to those tournaments because it meant I would be able to fight the best martial artists. I won many of the Grand Champion trophies. They were huge. I had to take them apart to get them in my car. I gave many of those away to family members when they visited from Mexico.

"WHITEY"

Master Richard always had his students competing against Master Sal's students. They both promoted LimaLama tournaments together. So, it seemed natural that their students would be competitive too. Master Richard had this one guy who was really good. Everyone called him "Whitey." Whitey had money and took private lessons with Master Richard. He was a brown belt. I had gone from blue belt, skipping green, and went straight to brown belt. When I tested for my brown, I was told I had to fight Whitey.

Because we were both in LimaLama, we normally would be matched against another martial art (karate, taekwondo). Not this time, Master Richard insisted on this fight, so it was done. It may have been pay-back for beating up his son. I don't really know, but it didn't matter, I wanted that brown belt. I fought Whitey, who was testing for his black belt. This event happened in Master Sal's garage. As soon as we did our salutations, we turned around to face each other and it was on! We went toe to toe. Neither of us backed up, and we never stopped. We kept going at it, hitting, kicking, punching, both of us landing hard shots but not backing off. Eventually, we were supposed to stop, but we ignored the calls to stop. We weren't sparring anymore, we were fighting. Literally, each of us trying to hurt the other.

Master Sal and Richard had to physically break us apart, but we were still trying to go after each other. Angrily, I told Master Sal in Spanish, "No me voy a dejar un pinche Gavacho que me pegen!" (I'm not going to let go of a fucking gringo that hits me.) Master Richard heard and understood what I had said about his student. But it was a good fight. Afterwards, we all went for dinner and Whitey invited me to hang out with him. As rich as that guy was, he had a lot of heart and respect for other fighters. He's what I called, "a white boy with a Mexican

THE BIRTH OF A WARRIOR

heart." You have to respect someone like that, regardless of their background. Eventually, we became friends and would go to tournaments together.

Back in the day, people would ask me about my opponent before a tournament: "Are you going to kick his ass?"

I always replied, "No, we're gonna kick some ass!" It was my way of showing respect for all fighters in the martial arts.

At tournaments, there were always some dudes who would go around pointing at people and saying, "I'm gonna kick his ass" or "I'm gonna do this or that to him," and then it never happened. They were just loudmouths! Some of the guys acted like roosters at tournaments. They talked a lot of trash, trying to intimidate opponents. They'd say stuff like, "I'm gonna fight you first, then you," pointing fingers at other participants, and then pointing to me, saying, "And I'm gonna fight you for first place." Cocky, like they were already taking the trophy home.

I'd stand up and tell them, "Fight me now!"

They'd respond, "No, no, no. I'm gonna fight you for first and second...."

Angrily, I'd interrupt. "No, no, no. Fuck that! Let's tighten this up now." I'd march straight to the tournament registration desk and tell them, "Forget about whoever you signed me up against. Put me with him now. I'll get rid of this loudmouth. Let him back it up now."

They couldn't back it up, they were all talk. I admit I was cocky in my youth, but never a loudmouth trying to start shit or intimidate opponents at tournaments. I did my talking in the ring with my fists. When confronted, most of those roosters would shut up and walk away. Those guys never lasted long in tournaments or the streets.

LIFE IS NOT A SPORT

Before LimaLama, I may have been considered to be just another young hard-headed street fighter from El Monte, California. There were many young men just like me in all the barrios of southern California. But luckily, I had found my place as a dedicated martial artist, a LimaLama devotee. I knew I was good because I constantly challenged myself and others, some without their consent, to test my abilities. Later, when I started teaching martial arts, I would remind my students before a tournament, "Fight! Don't try to score points, attack. But just don't hit the face." They would go on the mat aggressively and win because they were fighting. If they lost, it was usually because they did combinations and finished with a punch or kick to the head, drawing blood and getting disqualified. Other martial arts schools would complain about our LimaLama school, saying, "They're just fighting. They're not trying to score points. This is only a sport."

I'd reply, "To you it's a sport, but not in El Monte." In El Monte, we were all fighting. Fighting for our place in life. Life is not a sport.

I recall someone telling me about the meaning of the belts. Brown is the color of dirt; it brings you down to earth. Black belts are looking down at you as an up-and-coming threat. You need to be humble, but hungry too. Take your beatings, knowing you will someday join the black belt ranks. I had been fighting black belts as a brown belt. To me, reaching the level of a black belt only meant you have mastered *the basics* of that martial art style. A lot of guys would put their black belt certificates on the wall, and maybe start teaching students, but they stopped learning the art. In martial arts, there is always more to learn. There are many degrees of the art or other martial art styles that can be explored that broaden the mastery of your art. I didn't know it at the time, but I had internalized the

THE BIRTH OF A WARRIOR

Samurai bushido code that emphasized honor, courage, skill in martial arts, and loyalty to a warrior's master (daimyo) above all else. Little did I know it at the time, even the code would bring challenges I had not foreseen.

THE BUD BOYS

David Jimenez, Sal Jr. both in LimaLama and some other guys with good looking lowriders had started a car club called the "Bud Boys." They originally didn't tell me about the club because they were afraid I would try to take over. They were right; I always had ideas for events and fundraisers. I eventually joined them, but my car was a beat-up Ford Econoline van. It was ugly, so everyone called it "Cleopatra." But we loved that thing. We would fill it with food and beer and take off to the park, the beach, or the mountains. It was fun.

I was working for the City Parks and Recreation department during the summer. So, I told them I was taking a group of students to the mountains and the City Parks and Rec's program would pay for food and gas. My friends and I would go to the market and pick up whatever donations we could get and cook up the food for the Bud Boys parties. Not long after joining the Bud Boys, I was made vice-president.

I recall I was looking for work. I was a sophomore in high school. I went to this patio furniture store and applied for the job. The owner looked at me and said, "This is hard work. You won't last a week."

I told him, "I'll last two weeks; and if I don't last two weeks, don't pay me." He agreed. I kept that job for over a year. Later, I took my uncle there. He only lasted two months. I would take the leftover wood scraps to the high school wood shop, and we would make toys. The Bud Boys would sell them house-to-house in the neighborhood, and we'd use the money to go to Magic Mountain, the beach, or camping in the van. Like my

LimaLama training, I took everything as a challenge. Even if it was for pocket change, I wouldn't give up without a fight. I earned my money and was proud of it.

There were these two Girls Clubs, one from La Puente and the other from El Monte, that hated each other. They had become enemies over stupid shit. Finally, the fighting at school got so bad, two girls ended up going to the hospital. The president of the El Monte Girls Club lived on my street. The city, local police department, and both clubs wanted to put an end to the fighting. Because I was a youth counselor for the city and knew a few of the girls, I was recruited to help resolve the problems. I thought to myself, "this is a good chance to meet some girls and get paid too." I organized a dance in the community center with the Bud Boys. We planned a Battle of the Bands event with all the food and location costs donated by the city. The Bud Boys got to keep a percentage of the door fees. It was a great success.

The city wanted me to do the same with the gang, Monte Flores. I told them no, because gangs have no leader. I knew that the gangs do whatever they want to do, without a real leader. The car clubs had leaders, and all were careful not to get their vehicles involved in any territory disputes. Because most of us lived in different gang territories, all the youth were aware of the boundaries of living in the barrio. The city ignored my warning and sponsored another Battle of the Bands. As I predicted, a gang fight broke out, with one guy getting shot and many more injured and arrested.

The Bud Boys did agree to attend a city-sponsored retreat for the clubs. The city used a juvenile hall camp up in Azusa Canyon at Crystal Lake as the location for the retreat. The Girls Clubs stayed in separate cabins. The Bud Boys and a few other car club guys had their own cabin. It was a lot of fun, with no fights breaking out. We all participated in a football game

THE BIRTH OF A WARRIOR

against the Police Department. Man, did we kick ass, but I don't remember if we won or lost. I do remember getting hit so hard that my nose bled profusely before it stopped.

When I came back down from the higher altitude, the next day before school my nose started bleeding again. It wouldn't stop, and when my parents came home from work, they ended up calling for an ambulance. The cops were interrogating my mom and dad. "Does he do drugs? What kind of drugs is he currently using?" My parents were saying, "No, no drugs! He is a martial art fighter." The doctors said the only thing that saved me was my physical conditioning from being in martial arts. The doctors ended up singeing my nose vein to clot the leak. I stayed home for a few weeks recuperating.

GRANDMASTER WOO

Every martial arts school has something you can benefit from. Yet today many masters ignore new techniques when they are introduced to a new style or form. Martial art instructors know students' abilities and strengths differ. The more the student can learn, the better. It makes sense to share a multitude of techniques that a student can use, especially if the technique suits their size, strength, or physical limitations. The legendary Bruce Lee is a great example of this philosophy. He wanted to create an effective fighting style. He readily fused boxing, dance, Korean, Japanese, and other Chinese styles with Wing Chung and created a new art called, **Jeet Kune Do** (Way of the Intercepting Fist). Lee's martial arts philosophy emphasized practical fighting skill over rigid movements and patterns.

Likewise, GM Tino had the same intent, incorporating multiple martial art styles to create LimaLama. Jeet Kune Do and LimaLama masters readily accept the idea that their art form is always transforming. Some LimaLama schools today highlight Kenpo, lua, or kung fu techniques. Some LimaLama master's claim that their hybrid style is the best, and rightly so; they should say that, because it is what they know best. But the underlying LimaLama principles always remain constant, regardless of the school's name or fusion style.

As a young man, before and after I returned from military service, I routinely would visit other martial arts studios to observe their training regime. If they allowed visitors to participate, I would join for the day. Danny and I would find out what days the studios sparred and would show up. We would go to Shotokan and Kenpo schools to spar. The taekwondo school in Rosemead regularly allowed us to spar with their students. You weren't allowed to hit the face. But they threw so many kicks and angles that we learned how to block and counterstrike effectively. We'd then use this knowledge to train our students, and they'd use those techniques in tournament competition. After a while, Danny and I would flip a coin to see who would wear them out and who would finish them off. We were just having fun fighting.

I recall GM Jimmy Woo, the celebrated Sifu of Kung Fu San Soo, once challenged LimaLama. GM Woo had a school in El Monte. His students always wanted to fight guys in LimaLama. Some of the San Soo students were from my high school, and we would work out at the school gym. The San Soo students didn't compete in tournaments because they were told that San Soo was a deadly martial art and therefore prohibited from sparring competitions. We'd make fun of them about it, but we were curious too. We wanted to see them fight. It just so happened that Master Sal decided to have a tournament at El Monte High School and gave a flyer to one of GM Woo's students, Danny Cruz, who had been a regular visitor to our training sessions. It wasn't Master Sal's intent to challenge the kung fu, San Soo school. That would have been a grave disrespect to

THE BIRTH OF A WARRIOR

the Sifu grandmaster. Master Sal only meant to invite martial artists, like the San Soo students, to the competition.

Danny took the flyer to GM Woo to see if he would allow students to compete. GM Woo considered the flyer as a challenge against his dojo. He said, "I will fight. But we fight to the death." And when Master Sal was informed of Master Woo's response, he immediately responded, "No problem." The word got out about the dispute, and when I heard what had been said, I became angry.

I took it upon myself to visit the San Soo dojo. I wanted to see who had challenged my Master. I wanted to see what the big deal was about San Soo. A small part of me wanted to fight GM Woo to defend the honor of LimaLama. Looking back, it was a stupid idea; GM Woo would have killed me. Instead, I wisely sat and watched them train. But I admit if I had been challenged by anyone, I would have been ready to go toe to toe. I stayed for the whole class; and when approached about joining, I asked silly questions to cover up my real agenda. Of course, dojos are always try to recruit you. I just told them I'd think about it.

The word got out that I had gone to the kung fu, San Soo dojo. When Master Sal found out I had gone there, he knew instantly what my true intentions had been. He put me in the bull ring torture circle as punishment. Twelve students were surrounding me. Master Sal had me fight each one. I fought for about two minutes with each student. I knew Master Sal was going to fight me last. After I was physically spent, Master Sal stepped in the circle. I had to give him my best shots or he would have hurt me worse for holding back my attack. I went after him, and he just played with me. He kicked my ass. It was a reminder to me that the master decides who we fight and when it happens. It was a lesson to all his students to never assume you represent LimaLama unless he tells you. It was a lesson he would try to shove down my throat again years later.

GM Tino found out about the pre-tournament trash talk and told Master Sal, "Stop talking shit, or I'll go over there and kick both your asses." GM Tino never directly spoke to GM Woo about the matter out of respect for his peer. But GM Woo knew who GM Tino was in the martial arts community. Neither he nor Master Sal were willing to challenge GM Tino's ultimatum. That is how much respect—or fear—GM Tino commanded at the top echelon of martial artists at that time. The El Monte High School Tournament took place, and no San Soo students competed.

The San Soo guys I knew in high school always talked about how deadly San Soo was, as a reason why they didn't compete in tournaments. The claimed that they are trained to rip out the eye, bust your ribs, throat, and hit key vital organs to damage them. The problem with this belief is that they have no real proof. If you've been in a lot of fights, you will know what works and what doesn't work. But if you've never been in a fight, you don't know. You can hit a guy in the face or kick him across his kidneys and he might just laugh at you. Or worse, counter your attack and put you on the ground.

All martial art styles have some form of deadly or injurious strike techniques. But if you aren't practicing strikes, kicks, and counter attacks with an opponent, how can you know if your training is effective? In competition, fighters learn quickly to control their strikes so as not to maim, break or injure their opponents. More importantly, they learn how to fight effectively against someone who is trying to take their head off. Danny Cruz eventually left the San Soo studio and became a LimaLama student. We'd beat him up regularly in practice, but ultimately he did receive a black belt in LimaLama.

THE BIRTH OF A WARRIOR

I later read in one of GM Woo's books, where he said, "If I could get the speed and flexibility of the Limalama wrist to combine with San Soo, it wouldn't be authentic San Soo anymore. But it would be improved. It would be much more deadly. But then, San Soo would be bastardized." Unfortunately, some martial arts masters want to keep their styles so traditional that they don't improve it—for fighting—for fear of disrespecting the art.

In LimaLama, especially in Mexico, we have schools that have readily "bastardized" LimaLama, with the sole intent to improve the fighting style. Yet, LimaLama principles remain intact. Change always brings new ideas and forms. For me, training in LimaLama is akin to making a traditional family recipe for caldo (soup).

All caldos and martial arts are not the same. Yet, with each change in ingredients, the chef or Master seeks to improve their caldo, or fighting technique, just as my journey to learn different styles of martial arts was meant to improve my LimaLama fighting but never to turn away from it. The more I learned, the better I got in fighting. Whether it was boxing, Ba Qua, kickboxing, jiu-jitsu or muay Thai, it didn't matter the ingredient. I only wanted to win in martial arts tournaments, bathroom brawls, or bar fights. If I was a good fighter, then I would be honoring LimaLama for the world to see.

GANG BANGERS

One day I was wearing our Bud Boys sweater. It was blue with our logo "Bud Boys" with the letters "SGV," for San Gabriel Valley, under it, and my name above it. You weren't allowed to wear clothes with club or gang symbols on them on school grounds at El Monte High. But the word got around on campus that gang members were going to beat me up for "flying colors" at the school. I didn't care. I didn't think much about it, because I wasn't on school grounds and Bud Boys wasn't a gang. I was at the *Tasty Freeze* ice cream parlor across from the school waiting for some friends.

On hindsight, I shouldn't have worn the sweater. It invited trouble, but I didn't care. I knew a lot of the guys from that neighborhood. Those kinds of threats were often made by guys trying to make a name for themselves with their gang. My sweater made me an easy target for them. But I wasn't going to be intimidated.

My friends and I left to visit Mountain View High School, which was a new school that split up the students among El Monte High and the new high school. We loved it because guys could have a girlfriend at each school and the other girl would never find out. I didn't know it, but some Monte Flores gang members had followed us there. They were looking for me. They followed me because they had seen the Bud Boys Sweater I was wearing. We parked across the street, and my friends went on school grounds to meet some girls they knew.

I was hanging out across the street from the school when three gang members from Monte Flores started calling me out: "Fuck the Bud Boys!" "Bud Boys vale verga!" (suck dick), challenging me to fight. I wasn't concerned. Instead, I teased them about being a "flower." I told them, "Come on, three flowers? I'm so scared." One guy came towards me attempting to throw a punch. I moved forward to his right side to avoid the punch and threw a combination; right hand, left hook, and spinning back knuckle.

When I caught him with those shots, he dropped to the ground. The other two hoodlums had already run over at me too. I kicked the next guy in the stomach, and he hit the pavement. I then grabbed the first guy who was getting up and used him as a shield as the third dude tried to hit me. I kicked the second guy again who was on the ground. But one of them got

THE BIRTH OF A WARRIOR

a hold of my leg and knocked me down. I was hitting the guy on top of me while the other two guys started hitting me. Finally, my friends saw the commotion and came running over to help me. The "flower" gang saw them coming and ran off in their car to get away. Fight over, for now.

We didn't care about meeting any girls anymore, at least I didn't. These guys had gotten away. I was angry about the gang attack and wanted to get back at those guys for attacking me. Revenge is a bitter pill I would shortly have to swallow and learn from the hard way. Later that month, the Bud Boys had a party at the club president's family house. A lot of girls and guys from both schools came over. A guy from the Monte Flores gang showed up at the party. He was dating the president's sister. I confronted him. "Hey, you're one of the guys who tried to jump me." He tried to deny it. I told him, "You're not with your guys anymore. This is a Bud Boys party. You got to leave."

He responded, "Yeah, I know, but I'm seeing the girl who lives here…"

I told him, "No, you got to leave. Unless you go toe to toe with me." It didn't happen. The president and some other Bud Boys members stepped in and said to leave it alone. The president of the Bud Boys didn't want any problems at his family's house. That kind of neutralized it. I didn't want to ruin the party or my friend's home. Later, we decided to drive over to Tom's Burgers, a popular spot on Garvey and Central Avenue in El Monte. You could buy a dozen burgers for about $10. It was a popular hangout for all the teenagers in the area. The guy from the Monte Flores gang went too, following our group in his car.

Some other dudes showed up from another local gang and started arguing with him. We stepped in and told them all to "Drop it, forget about it," that we weren't gang members and didn't want any problems. We told the guy who was dating the

Bud Boys president's sister, "That's enough, get in the car. Let's just get out of here." Instead, the guy went to his car, got out a gun, and started shooting—pow, pow, pow—at the other gang. Everyone scattered and we jumped in our cars, taking flight to be safe. We wanted to forget about the incident, but we realized that the street gang thought the Bud Boys had fired the weapon on them. Now I had two gangs giving me problems.

After that dumb incident, I still hadn't shook off my burning desire to get payback on the Monte Flores gang for trying to jump me. I wanted to get even; the gang had disrespected me, and I wanted some kind of closure. So, about a week later, I went looking for them. I went to each guy's house I knew about in El Monte. I recall knocking at one of the houses and the father, a veterano from the gang, answered the door. He was plastered with tattoos and had that old-school cholo way of talking. It was only then I realized the whole family probably had the gangster mentality. I asked if so-and-so lived there, and he responded, "What do you want with my son?"

I told him, "Your son tried to jump me, I'm here and I want to go toe to toe."

He looked at me. "Well, what if I don't let you? What if I pull out my gun and just shoot you?"

I replied, making eye contact, "No, I don't think you would do that. Eventually we are going to run into each other. He tried to get me with two other guys. But I'm here by myself. Sí, tiene huevos, que salga!" (If he has balls, come out.).

The father called his son outside and we fought. I kicked the shit out of him. I wasn't really hurting him, but I was totally dominating him. The father said, "That's enough, shake hands now." We shook hands. The Monte Flores gang member's jefito (father) looked at me and said, "Tiene huevos. I like that. Where are you from?"

THE BIRTH OF A WARRIOR

I responded, "I don't belong to nobody. That's what I tried to tell your son." The next couple of days, I went to the next gang member's house and then the next. They all got their licks in, they hit me—but that's what made it good—I got even in a fair fight. None of them could beat me; instead I gave them a beating. After fighting each one, I felt that we were now even, and they would leave me alone. I had gotten my revenge, but did it respectfully, mano-a-mano. I was naive. The concept of a fair fight doesn't translate well with the gang mentality. Little did I know that I had just opened the door for more trouble.

BECOMING AN ARMY GRUNT

Around 1993, Chuck Norris formed a team called the LA Stars. This was a team of black belts that were going to fight in Hawaii in one of the first full-contact tournaments. Danny Esquivel had tried out for it. He lost to a guy named Lenny Ferguson, from the Black Karate Federation. I was still a brown belt, but I had beaten Lenny before in two different tournaments. I watched how Lenny defeated Danny to make the LA Stars team. That was how I learned to fight Danny. Danny and I would go toe to toe every time we fought. After a while, we just couldn't spar together because we'd hurt each other. We'd fight so hard, doing the same things to each other. I had better flexibility and was a lot faster. Danny was stronger and had more experience. But I always gave him a run for his money.

Cecil Peoples, one of the pioneers of kickboxing, had fought with the LA Stars. There was a lot of attention given to the team and the upcoming Hawaiian tournament. It was a big deal among all the fighters in the martial arts community. I knew I could compete with these black belts but had not been allowed to test for my black belt. I tried to get Master Sal to let me "borrow" a black belt just to compete. But he wouldn't let me go. I suspect, because his son hadn't qualified for the tournament, he didn't want to embarrass him by allowing me to compete. The team included Benny Urquidez and Blinky Rodriguez from the Jet Center. Benny's brother Arnold was also attending as the trainer. The three of them were well-known champion fighters in full contact and kickboxing.

I was upset by Master Sal's decision not to let me compete for the LA Stars. I knew I was capable of winning and felt cheated by not having the chance to compete. At this point in my life, I had experienced too many roadblocks for success in my way. Master Sal never opened a real martial arts studio that I could proudly claim as my school. Moreover, he wouldn't test me for black belt even though I sparred and trained them for him. I decided I needed to find another direction for my life. I didn't want to be teaching martial arts in churches, community centers, or garages anymore. I wanted a real commercial school. Even though I was still a brown belt, I wanted a real martial arts school that could showcase LimaLama and would prosper. That vision stayed with me from that day forward.

Unfortunately, my problem with the Flores Gang finally caught up with me. A month after I had fought those three dudes, the gang shot up my neighbor's house in retaliation for me going after them. They'd mistakenly thought it was my house. It was chicken shit the way they did it, a drive-by cowardly act. The fights were just between them and me. Why did they need to retaliate? My neighbors and family had nothing to do with it. I told myself, *Fuck this, I'm not bringing my family into the middle of this mess. My ego got me into trouble. My need for revenge put my family and neighbors at risk. Those maricones shot up the wrong house. It could have been my house, injuring my brother, sister, or parents.*" At that moment, I decided I had to leave El Monte to protect them. My father half-heartedly advised me to go to Mexico, but he knew I would figure a way out of the mess on my own. I decided to join the military.

THE BIRTH OF A WARRIOR

I had already been thinking about it. I could have gone to Mexico; my older brother had already gone south of the border before. He wanted to join the service when he was in high school because he was falling behind in class. My parents didn't give him permission and sent him to study in Mexico. Instead of going to school, he ended up working. By the time he came back to the states, he was further behind. He ended up having a lot of catching up to do before he finished his education. That was one reason why I didn't really want to go to Mexico. I saw no real future there.

I visited the Recruiting Office at the El Monte Mall. At first, I wanted to go in the Air Force. Everyone told me that they had better training, better food, and housing. But it was gonna take me three months to get in, and I wasn't gonna wait that long. Then I considered joining the Marines. Everybody talked highly of them; uniforms, attitude—the few, the proud—you know the drill. But the Marine recruiter was too gung-ho. Something just didn't click with me. I liked the presentation, but I wanted more facts. I asked him, "How soon can I leave?" And he replied, "Can you leave tomorrow?" That response just didn't fit well with me. I wanted nothing to do with the Navy; I preferred my feet on the ground. Finally, I went to the Army recruiter. He was pretty cool. Showed me the recruitment tape, shared some of the highlights and locations. I told him, "Let me think about it." He immediately tried to get me to sign. I wasn't convinced.

The guys I hung out with all talked about going into the service, maybe, working our way up to Special Forces, Rangers, or Green Berets. My brother-in-law had just missed the Vietnam war. He figured he could get into computers, and the Army could teach him. He assumed he'd be in an office working on computers, and not a soldier out on patrol. Then, when he got out of the service, he could easily get a job. It was a perfect plan.

The recruiter said, "Sure we got computers." They sent him to Europe and put him in a tank. Tanks have computers. I learned from his sad experience to not accept the word of any recruiter. I had a choice; go with the Army to Germany, Europe, or Korea; or, since I was into the martial arts, go to Okinawa, Japan. The Marines were willing to send me there too.

I asked my LimaLama students their opinion about military service; many had served in the Marine Corps. Nine out of 10 of them told me not to go with the Marines. They claimed the Marines got paid less and got treated worse. *Yeah*, I thought, *"the proud and few."* All I knew was that the Air Force bombed from the sky, Navy bombed from the sea, and Marines were the first to land and fight. The Army cleaned up and backed up the Marines. All the branches had their good and bad points. In the end, military service was about giving your life away to country for a few years. I had to choose.

I also had trained many police officers. They said, "Lorenzo, you should be a cop. Join the LAPD or Sheriff's Department. I looked into it and found out I didn't meet the criteria. They had a height requirement, and I didn't have my citizenship papers. You had to be a citizen and all I had was a green card. At the time, I was unwilling to give up my Mexican citizenship because I feared not being able to buy property in Mexico. I didn't know you could get dual citizenship back then. The bottom line for me was that I needed to get out of El Monte. I chose the Army. I didn't feel I needed to prove myself to anyone. I already had proven myself as a fighter on the streets and in martial arts tournaments.

I told my older brother, Hector, that I had signed up. I showed him my papers, with a reporting date of October 31, 1974, Halloween day. He immediately went and signed up too. Unlike a few years before, he didn't need permission from my parents anymore because he was of age. He could make his own

THE BIRTH OF A WARRIOR

choice. My parents were angry with me. They blamed me for his signing up to join the Army. He left two weeks before me. I remember my father cried. It was the first time I ever saw him cry. As my brother drove away, my parents turned and looked at me, never saying a word. I realized it was my fault for all the bad that had been brought upon us at that moment.

My close friend Alejandro Perez and I both were scheduled for Army pick up at 3:00 p.m. He never trained in martial arts. He was more of an artist. He was a Bud Boys member and had a Chevy Vega he called "Lulu." In fact, about twelve other guys we knew from the Buds and martial arts training also went into the service. Everyone shipped off to different places. My brother was supposed to go to Fort Ord in California but ended up going to Fort Polk in Louisiana. At the time, I thought only Perez and I ended up at Fort Ord. We knew, once we signed on the dotted line, that we didn't belong to ourselves anymore. We were government property and expendable. When I got to the basic training camp at Fort Ord, they gave me E3 designation because of my recruitment of the other guys that joined from our El Monte group. Private Perez and I were now government issue. The Army would tell us what to do for the next few years.

3

HONING THE SWORD

CHARLIE COMPANY ENFORCER

BASIC COMBAT TRAINING IS the introduction to Army service, where I was going to learn the traditions, tactics, and methods of becoming a soldier. I was ready and willing to learn. Master Sal had trained me hard, lots of drills and exercises, to prepare me for military life without him realizing it. I had no doubts about what lay ahead at boot camp. I thought to myself, "Hey, I've gone through so much already. What is the Army going to do that hasn't been done to me?" I was totally wrong about that thought.

My mom bought me new clothes. She didn't want me going to the Army wearing my old clothes. She treated it like it was my first day in grade school or I going to visit family in Mexico. She wanted me to make a great impression. It didn't matter. The Army put all the recruits' civilian clothing in storage. I wouldn't see my new clothes again until the end of basic training.

Most of the guys had gotten *high* and *tight* haircuts before arriving at the camp. It didn't matter, the Army took the rest of our hair away too. They put us in recruit military uniforms sporting short, cropped heads and army boots. They were making it clear—physically—that we all were going to look the same and very soon act the same. We were no longer civilians we were *ground pounders*, training to become soldiers.

Perez and I were in Charlie Company. The drill sergeants did exactly as we expected. They pushed us to our limits—not so much physically, but they intended to challenge us mentally. They were trying to break us. I knew that. Perez knew that too. The drill sergeants would bark orders to dig fox holes right here. Pointing to a spot on a hill. Then when everyone had dug the holes, they'd bark out, "Cover these holes, now." It made no sense to dig holes with no purpose. But we suspected that they wanted to see who would complain or worse, refuse. We were learning, the hard way, through forced labor, to follow orders without questioning authority.

Perez and I were housed in the same barracks. I convinced the platoon leader to give us one of the private rooms in the barracks. My future E3 designation that I would earn at graduation might have given me an advantage. The platoon leader told us, "As long as you keep it clean and inspections are up to par, you can keep the room. But, if either of you get a demerit, you're out. We'll put someone else in it." Perez and I made sure to keep that room GI (Government Issue) clean.

Two weeks after we had arrived at the base, Perez came back to our room in the late afternoon, looking like he had been in a fight. I could see some bruising around his neck and arms, and his clothes looked disheveled. I asked him what happened. He tried to hide the painful look on his face by turning away, and said, "Don't worry about it. Don't get involved."

"I am involved. We came into the service together. There's no secrets between us, man. What happens to you happens to me too."

Perez looked at me, thought for a second, and then told me what had happened. He had accidently bumped into some tall white guy inside the barracks latrine as he was walking out. The guy grabbed Perez and slammed him into the wall. He physically threatened Perez and pulled out a martial arts membership card that said he was a brown belt. He was trying to intimidate Perez with his skill level. After Perez finished telling the story, I told him, "Okay, I'll be right back."

I immediately left the room and went to the room of the platoon leader. The tall white guy was the squad's leader. I knocked on the door and he answered, "Come in." I entered the room and shut the door behind me. He was by himself. I looked at him and said, "Hey, my partner told me that you're into the martial arts. I know some martial arts. He said that you showed him a membership card. What is the card?"

He replied, "Well, I'm a brown belt."

I don't recall now what style he had trained in, and at that moment I really didn't care. I responded, "Do you think you can teach me?"

"If I show you, I'm going to have to really do it to you. I'm going to have to hit you!"

Smiling to myself, I thought, *"Perfect!"* I remained calm and responded, "Oh really? No problem, if that's the way you teach. Maybe, if I feel it, I will learn it better."

As I spoke, I saw him start to stretch. He was limbering up and started removing his boots. So, I started to copy him and took off my boots. When he was ready, he got into a martial arts stance, one leg back and one forward, with his hands up. I asked him, "Now what?"

He answered, "Oh, you have to copy me."

"What are you doing?" I responded naively, as if I'd never seen the stance before. He then shared with me the Japanese word for his karate stance. "What does that mean?"

"Look, just put your hands up." He was becoming impatient with my questions.

As instructed, I put my hands up in a fighting stance.

"Now, what I want you to do is take a step and punch me. I'm going to show you a technique."

Without hesitation, I quickly took a step forward and boom, boom, boom. He never got to show me any technique as I blocked his punch with a strike to his bicep and chest, bouncing him off the wall and dropping him to the ground. I jumped on top of him and started working his body with my fists. I didn't want to hit the face or leave any bruises. I used "drop" punches, slapping or cupping my wrist as I delivered shots to his body and arms. He wasn't trying to hit me; he was trying to protect his body from my shots.

He got the pain effect, even though I wasn't trying to break any ribs. If I had left bruises or busted his lip or nose, then he could bring charges against me. He was the platoon leader; the Army brass would take his word over mine. So, I intentionally busted him up just enough to hurt him and made sure to leave no marks or injuries.

He didn't know what hit him. He thought I was going to throw a punch and leave it out there, so he could hit me and do his technique. His mistake was that he told me to hit him. So I did, repeatedly.

As I stood over him, I told him, "The next time you try any shit with Perez or anybody else in our company, I'm going to seriously work you." He knew what I meant. He never said a word as I put my boots on and left the room.

When I got back to my room, Perez was sitting on his bunk staring at me. I knew he was dying to find out and finally asked, "What happened, Lorenzo?"

I wouldn't share any details of the assault, but I told him, "Before a minute is up, that dude is going to knock on the door, and he's gonna want me to train him."

Sure enough, there was a knock on the door. Perez said, "You got to be kidding me!"

I opened the door, and the big white dude looked at me and shook his head. "Oh, man. What did you do to me, man? My chest hurts, my ears hurt, all my shit hurts. You must have trained in something. Can you teach me?"

I looked at him and said, "I don't go around flashing any membership card. But if I hear that you're flashing that card or you're bullying any of the other guys, I'm going to fuck you up. For one thing, I'm not teaching you because you're a bully. Secondly, I don't like many people that are taller than me, and that's almost everybody. You can go now."

From that day forward, he started acting nicer to everybody else. Eventually, the word got out about what happened to him. The squad found out that I was the one that had put the hurt on him. It didn't take long for me to be considered Charlie Company's champ. I had been anointed as the barracks enforcer.

It seemed when a private was granted leave, his leave would be cancelled because someone reported a rule or regulation violation he supposedly committed. Some dudes snitched because they were jealous or simply didn't like the guy. The problem for the rest of us was that the sergeants punished the whole platoon for the infraction. And I didn't need any more stupid hills to climb or holes to dig. Guys would come over and ask me if I could take care of it. So, when we would all be marching or running to the gunnery range, I'd hand my rifle to Perez and go beat up the snitch. The tunnels to the beach or rifle range ran underneath the freeway, so that is where I'd go after the snitches. There would be no witnesses.

One guy I busted up was hurt so bad that when we went to the rifle range and were coming back, the poor guy was barely just coming out of the tunnel. Another time, the Army had pogo sticks and we used them to run an obstacle course. I would always volunteer to get the sticks. As we got to the tunnel, I would turn around on my targeted snitch and throw a kick to the face or chest. Our drill sergeant eventually found out it was me. He may have spotted me coming out of the tunnel, because he sent me to report to the HQ (Headquarters) office the same day.

MAD DOG AND THE WRESTLER

The sergeant was a Vietnam veteran, with a nickname of "Mad Dog." He suffered from post-traumatic stress disorder, PTSD. We'd be running in formation with our M16s, and all of a sudden he'd freak out, yelling "Everyone get down! Gooks! Gooks!" Other Field Sergeants would arrive, ordering us to get up and get to the range. They would calmly talk to him and bring him down from his mental hysteria.

By this time, I had only been in basic training for a month when Sergeant "Mad Dog" had me report to his office. There were some other sergeants in the office with him too. He wanted to go toe to toe with me. He called me *maggot*, *scum*, or *wetback*, just to piss me off. He tried to convince me to show him some martial arts moves. I told him, "I don't know nothing." He wouldn't believe me. He told me he heard that I was the enforcer for our company and that I had training in martial arts.

Finally, I told him. "Sergeant. Sir, It's a no-win situation for me. If I tell you I know martial arts, then you are going to test me. If I were to fight you, win or lose, I lose. So, no matter what I say or do, I can't win. I can't fight you."

No words were said. Sergeant Mad Dog looked at the other sergeants in the room, and I was quickly dismissed. But I ended up getting reassigned to Kitchen Patrol duty, or "KP," as it's called in the Army. I would be spending time cleaning pots and pans, peeling potatoes, and mopping.

My KP sergeant had already heard about my situation and asked me questions about my martial arts education. I ended up training him in LimaLama to reduce my kitchen duty assignments. He was cool. He liked the way I trained him. We became good friends during my boot camp days. The platoon companies took the physical training tests a few weeks later. I was two points short of the maximum score. One guy in the platoon aced it: he got the maximum score, which was really rare. He was in great shape.

We finally got our first leave, but it was restricted to the base. We couldn't go off base into the city to party and meet girls, so we went drinking at the base pub that had benches outside. The beer is not that strong on base, but we could buy more of it for the price. There was a guy who was a wrestler, and he wanted to grapple with me. I told him, "No, I don't wrestle."

So, he said, "I'll tell you what: Let's trade punches."

I nodded, "Sure, put some money on the table." Everybody then began comparing martial arts and wrestling. Some said, "The wrestler will win because he's in better shape." He got more confident, hearing all the comments, and agreed to the bet. We bet cash.

The wrestler stood up in front of me. "Come on, see if you can take my best punch."

"All right." I got in a semi-circle, horse stance. He wound up and *Boom!* hit me to the stomach as hard as he could. I took the shot without flinching. So, I was standing there as the crowd got quiet. He prepared himself for my turn to throw a punch. And I quickly shot a drop punch right to his solar plexus. *Pow!* He went down to his knees. He struggled to breathe. It took him awhile to get his breath back. Everyone started "jaw-jacking" him for talking smack and taking the stupid bet. But he stubbornly stuck to his belief that wrestling is still better than martial arts. I didn't care; I picked up the money, put it in my pocket, and left.

BATTLE WITH BRAVO COMPANY

Basic training was finally completed. Before we deployed to our post assignments, I got some leave time to visit my family. I went home to test for my black belt and the initiation into the black belt brotherhood. My parents went to watch the ceremony. I easily completed the black belt test. Part of the initiation included getting hit by all the black belts. The first guy in line to hit me was Master Sal, who kicked me in the stomach. Then his son, Danny, came up and struck me in the chest.

The other twelve black belts formed a line and wanted to hit me too, but I squared off in a fighting stance and told them, "Hey, if your gonna hit me, I'm gonna hit back."

Master Sal got angry and told me, "It was tradition."

I responded, "Well traditions are made to be broken. These guys aren't hitting me without a fight." Master Sal was pissed off at me and my stubborn pride. Maybe it was ego. I don't know. In my mind, Master Sal and his son, Danny, had my respect. They were true warriors. These other black belts would have to fight me if they wanted to punch me.

My parents didn't understand what was happening. I later explained to my father what had happened at the black belt ceremony. And he said, "Hey, you're not in a gang. That's what gangs do." He was right. Unfortunately, I never received my certificate from Master Sal. I was treated as a black belt among my peers and wore a black belt at tournaments. But having the actual black belt certificate in my hand never happened. It was kept from me for pissing off Master Sal. Years later, I received my 2nd through 8th degree ranks from Grandmaster Tino when I trained directly under him.

When I returned to Fort Ord, we started our training for the jobs we would eventually be assigned. I already knew I was going to Korea. Before I joined, the recruiter had informed me I could either pick my location or a job. If I wanted both, then I'd have to sign up for four years. I picked the location, Korea. I was hoping I could find time to learn some Asian martial arts while there. We had weekend leave, and this guy named Valdez was going to be picked up by a friend, so Perez and I joined him. He was headed to Santa Cruz to party. We had a good time in Santa Cruz.

When we got back to the base, we found the wrestler dude I had the punching duel with, beaten up and lying on his bunk in the barracks. Supposedly, someone in Bravo Company kicked his ass. Before anyone in the barracks could figure out what had happened, our drill sergeant barged into the barracks, barking out loud as he was touring the barracks, "In my day, if somebody turned around and got beat up, we got even. Nobody in my platoon, my company, my squad gets their ass kicked! We're Charlie Company."

After the sergeant left, we scrambled over to the wrestler to find out what had happened. He said he was at the base pub and decided to wrestle some guy from Bravo Company for money. He said, "I beat the guy, but he didn't have any money. He spent it all on beer, and I guess he figured he could get more beer money from beating me. So, I went after him, but this other guy stepped in and said, 'You're not fighting him.' So, then we start fighting, and the guy kicked my ass."

I looked at him. "Listen, I'm going after the guy from Bravo Company, but you have to pay me."

Another private chimed in, "That dude you beat didn't even have money, and this is what was done to you?"

The wrestler looked dejected, so I reminded him, "Your lucky we already passed the PT test. If not, it's an automatic recycle. You'd have to do the whole basic training over again."

The wrestler, nodding in agreement, looked directly at me. "I'll give you $200 if you'll take care of it."

It wasn't my ego or any newfound loyalty to Charlie Company that motivated me to fight. The way I figured it; I was going to be able to get more martial arts practice. Somebody would get to hit me, and I would get to hit back. Whether I won or lost, I'd get paid. So, I happily agreed to the deal.

At Fort Ord, the only time I had to practice was in my room. Perez didn't mind it. But my practice was limited to about one hour a day. The wrestler gave me the cash, and the word quickly got out on base. Everyone knew—Bravo Company was going to the back of one of the secluded buildings on base, and Charlie Company was going to meet them for a fight.

In hindsight, we figured the drill sergeant took advantage of the wrestler's fight dilemma. The sergeant's convenient tour through the barracks at the time we were all returning from leave was intended to instigate a brawl between the companies. Everyone on base knew why, when, and where the fight was to occur. They could have easily stopped us, but I think they wanted to see a fight.

The Army brass knew I was the enforcer for Charlie Company, but they just couldn't prove it. I'm fairly sure the KP sergeant had told them about my LimaLama background and training. I didn't care at this point, because I was making some money out of the mess and admittedly looking forward to battling Bravo Company's best fighter. The consequences for my actions be damned!

The banter from all the Army ground pounders was getting louder and louder as we turned the corner behind the barracks and saw Bravo Company waiting for us. Everybody was yelling slurs at each other. We must have looked like a bunch of sharks before the feeding frenzy would begin. I looked across at our enemy and told the wrestler, "Show me the guy." He pointed to the dude in the front. I started laughing.

The wrestler looked at me. "What's so funny?"

"Don't worry about it." I turned to face the circus crowd. "Everyone just stand back!" Charlie Company knew I was about to go toe to toe with Bravo Company's chicken-shit grunt. They stood quietly, as instructed, and I started walking forward alone.

My Bravo enemy, not much bigger than me, began walking slowly towards me too. He had the same look I did. No fear, just ready to strike. It reminded me of a gunfight in the movies, except, at this moment, we would be slinging punches and kicks, not bullets. As we were getting closer, both companies grew totally silent. The tension in the air was thick. As I approached within punching range, I reached out my hand, and my opponent reached out his too. We shook hands, laughing and hugging ferociously. It was Danny Esquivel, Master Sal's son. I told him, "Come on Danny, Charlie Company will buy you a beer." I turned to the wrestler and said, "If you couldn't handle me, you sure weren't going to beat my master's son." Both companies were shocked at the outcome. But everyone soon relaxed and ended up together at the base pub, both companies getting drunk on the wrestler's dime.

THE "RINGER" OF SOUTH KOREA

I could not wait to ship out to Korea. When I finally boarded a civilian plane to our destination, I was fortunate to meet an important person. He was wearing civilian clothes and sat next to me. I was wearing my Army private uniform. It was a long flight, and he asked me where I was from and what my training was in for the Army. I soon realized he was the Commanding

Officer, Major Cherry, for the base at Pyeongtaek, Korea, 249 MP Detachment, close to the OSAN Air Force Base. He was curious about my martial arts background, and I guess he took a liking to me because he made sure I was assigned to his company. Eventually, he started taking lessons in LimaLama from me during my tour of duty in Korea.

I couldn't wait to find a martial arts dojo in South Korea. They mostly taught forms of Moo Duk Kwan, taekwondo, and hapkido, and all involved a lot of kicking. Here in the states, many people claimed that taekwondo was more of a sport and not a fighting martial art. Practitioners would be angry about the claim, but there was some truth to it. I had never lost a tournament fight to a taekwondo fighter. I mean no disrespect to the art, but a lot of taekwondo techniques useful in tournaments or sparring are not conducive to real fights in close-quarter situations like house parties, nightclub bars, and public bathrooms. But that doesn't mean they can't knock your head off.

I later learned, after I returned to the United States, that there was another Korean style called *Hwa Rang Do*, known as "The Way of the Flowering Knights." It was a comprehensive Korean martial art that was developed in the 1960s by Sifu Joo Bang Lee and his brother Joo Sang Lee. It has multiple areas of focus, including stand-up fighting with open-hand striking, weapons, throws and takedowns, and some ground fighting. But it is also an internal martial art style that also teaches different types of meditative and healing practices, intellectual and character development, and artistic pursuits. Sifu Lee was a real fighter.

I recall competing in one of Sifu Joo Bang Lee's tournaments in Westminster, California, around 1978–79, after my return to civilian life. I was fighting this guy and I did an axe kick on his head, almost knocking him out. But somehow, on impact, my leg muscle knotted up and I hit the mat. I couldn't get back up.

Sifu Lee came over and slapped his hands together and rubbed them for heat, just like the character Mr. Miyagi did in the movie, *Karate Kid*. Sifu Lee lifted my gi and began to massage my thigh, and I heard a *Pop*. He somehow put whatever had locked up my lower spine and leg, back where it belonged.

I was able to continue fighting and won Grand Champion that day. I was surprised that Sifu Joo Bang Lee knew so much about the healing and spiritual side of martial arts, and I was grateful for his assistance that day. On reflection, I realized that my Army service experience in Korea benefited my LimaLama techniques and style of fighting immensely. But when I was serving in Korea, I was only interested in learning to fight better, instead of trying to learn the internal arts.

The Army base at Pyeongtaek, Korea, had physical fitness programs, like weightlifting and boxing, for enlisted personnel. During my tour of duty, I learned that US Air Force General Curtis LeMay, while in charge of the Strategic Air Command in the early 1950s, instituted the first widespread US military effort to incorporate Asian martial arts into regular military training. He is credited with recruiting leading Japanese judo, karate, and aikido experts to train on American bases. Luckily for me, one of the programs at the Pyeongtaek Army base was taekwondo.

Every military base in foreign countries has a black belt instructor. That is one way the local martial arts masters could earn a living. I'd ask a guy who had gotten his black belt while in military service, how long they had been training, and he'd say, "Oh, about a year and a half." But when we'd spar, they all sucked at it. They were too mechanical in their movements, and they had no power in their strikes. I called them, "GI black belts." In my opinion, they had bought their belts. They didn't earn them. But there were a few exceptions. Some really good black belts came out of the service. A good example was Chuck

Norris, who had received his black belt while serving in the military and became a world recognized karate champion.

The sifu instructor was a Korean gentleman from the local village who contracted with the base to teach Army personnel who were interested in learning martial arts. I immediately joined up to learn a new fighting art. The other students were brand new, not knowing even how to tie the uniform gi belt. I showed them how to tie the belt correctly. The sifu never arrived for our first training class.

Instead, a red belt (equivalent to brown belt in karate) instructor was going to lead the class. He was a large white guy, weighing about 220 pounds, over six foot tall, from the Army base. He had been training in Korean taekwondo for some time. There were about 10 students, all of us privates from the base. He lined us all up facing him. He stood in front of the farthest student in the line and told him to throw a punch as he stood in front of him. I assumed he would be showing us a technique. The first guy threw a punch and was immediately kicked to the ground. He moved on to the next guy and did another technique, knocking him down to the ground too.

I realized his intent was not to teach, rather only to just show off his kicking talent or intimidate us. I wasn't sure what I should do. I didn't want to expose my martial arts background to others. I was in a quandary. Should I let him hit me or not? Each time he knocked someone down, I could feel my body resisting and my mind quickly focusing on a decision. By the time he got to me, he had already knocked everyone else to the floor.

I decided then, I wasn't going to be one of them. As he stood in front of me, he smiled like he knew what was going to happen. He was wrong; he had picked the wrong guy to bully. I quickly stepped forward, throwing multiple combinations and knocking him to the ground. I jumped on top of him and threw more shots to the head and body before I stopped. My intent was not to stop him but to hurt him. I was angry at his conceit. Like sheep among the wolves, the other students just watched in shock. When I was done, he was in bad shape. In my anger, I had broken his ribs and his jaw and inflicted multiple contusions to his face. I found out later that he was a sergeant at the Army base.

When the taekwondo sifu on base found out what had happened to his red belt instructor, he notified Major Cherry, the camp commander. I spoke with the sifu and tried to explain what had occurred. But he kept shaking his head, saying in broken English, "You a ringer, you a ringer." I didn't understand what he meant. Then he showed me a *Karate Illustrated* magazine with a picture of me and Danny Esquivel on the cover. I realized then what he meant by "ringer." I already belonged to a martial arts school and therefore, according to Korean martial arts tradition, if you belong to a school, you must remain with that martial arts school. You cannot change fight schools without your master's permission. He gave me my money back for the training, telling me, "I cannot teach you, you a professional. You go somewhere else."

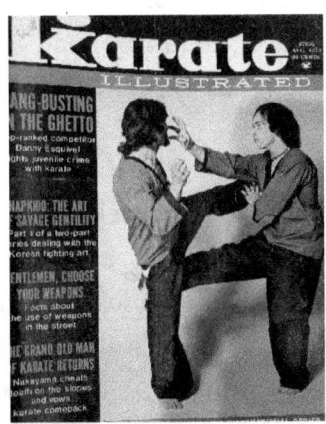

August 1974 Karate Illustrated, *showing Lorenzo Rodriguez (L) and Danny Esquivel (R).*

The next morning, I was called to the base commander's office. Commander Cherry was pissed off and wanted to hear from me directly about what had happened. I explained what had occurred and why I decided to hit back. He said, "You know you cannot hit a superior officer. You can be court-martialed for hitting and injuring the sergeant."

"Commander, may I speak freely, sir?" Commander Cherry nodded in the affirmative.

"Commander, I didn't know he was a sergeant. Besides, this occurred while we both were off duty."

Commander Cherry shook his head. "Lorenzo, you're in the United States Army. You are never off duty. Yours is a 24-hour-a-day obligation."

All I could say was, "Yes, sir," as I looked down at the floor. I realized I was fucked. I told myself, "*Why did I beat this guy down? Why didn't I stop sooner? Why didn't I just let him hit me?*"

Commander Cherry studied my face for a moment before he spoke, "Lorenzo, I will make this go away. Other students in the class have already lodged complaints about his actions too. But you can't be hitting any superior officers, or you can be damn sure you'll be in the stockade and court-martialed next time. Do you understand me, soldier?"

I snapped to attention, held my head high, and said, "Yes, sir!" I knew I had gotten really lucky that day!

BA GUA QUAN

In California. I could visit other schools or dojos and spar or train with them. I never intended to leave LimaLama; I simply wanted to learn other fighting styles and techniques. In Korea, I was hoping to get that opportunity. Unfortunately, it didn't matter what I wanted. In this sifu's eyes, I was a "ringer." I was no longer welcome in his school. At the time, I had no idea that he told other dojo masters in the village about what had

HONING THE SWORD

happened on base. I would soon learn that this "ringer," would not be allowed in their dojos either.

In Asia, the tradition has always been that if you train with one martial arts master, you remain with that master. You are demonstrating loyalty to that martial art. If you decide to move to another master, you must first get permission from your master. In some cases, you had to be introduced by a student to their master before he would consider you. In the states, I never encountered this kind of practice.

I began visiting Korean dojos in the local villages. I always wore civilian clothes. I knew if I went in my gi, they would consider that as a challenge. I would always pay my respects. They ask you to bow, and I would bow. I wasn't used to bowing, because in LimaLama we don't bow. We pay respect by bringing our hand from our heart out to show the world our empty hands. But I was willing to ignore my own martial art style—while in the service—to be accepted by a Korean master.

Upon entering a dojo, I would ask where the visitors sit. I would quietly watch the class train to see if it were an art form I would be interested in learning. After a short time, I would see a student jog over and whisper to the sifu, and both would look in my direction. The senior student would then walk over to the exits and close the door and lock it. I can only guess that they believed I was there to steal their techniques or Kata styles. They were not going to allow me to leave without teaching me a lesson for disrespecting their dojo. They perceived my action of visiting their dojo as a challenge.

I did not want trouble, I only wanted to find another dojo to continue my training. But as the sifu from the base had said, I was a "ringer" and not welcome. He probably had spread the word to his peers about me. I knew I had to fight my way out. This happened about four different times at different dojos. The sifu would never fight me, the advanced students were expected to do the dirty work. A few of the faster students got their licks in, but I got mine too. It was never a fair fight. I ended up fighting two or three guys each time. After I knocked down a few, the sifu would tell his students to stop. They would give up fighting and open the door for me to leave.

It was frustrating for me not to be able to find a place to train in a martial art style. That was why I chose to go to Korea. I wanted to learn something new. Finally, a guy on base told me about a sifu at the local Pyeongtaek village. The sifu didn't advertise to the public. All his students came by word of mouth. He was originally from China and taught Ba Gua Quan martial arts from his home. It was not far from the base, so I went to check it out. The dojo looked like a large barn, right at the outskirts of the village.

Though there are many stories and versions of how Ba Gua was founded, the most widely accepted version is that Dong Hai Chuan (1798–1879), a native of Zhujiawu, south of Wenan County in Hebei Province in Northern China, was the founder of Ba Qua. I later learned that Ba Gua Quan (also known as Pa Kua Chuan) was one of the three major internal Chinese martial arts.

I didn't understand the difference in names or styles. It didn't matter. I was happy to have found a sifu who would accept me as a student. I was about to discover a Chinese martial art in a Korean village.

As I entered the place, all eyes fell upon the non-Asian visitor. I approached this Chinese man, who I surmised was the sifu by his dress and mannerisms. I remember, he calmly stood watching my every movement as I approached him. I offered my respects and introduced myself. I explained I wanted to learn from him. I told him I was a black belt in LimaLama. There was a guy there who translated what I said in Chinese.

Sifu asked why I wanted to learn Ba Qua, and I explained I wanted to learn to fight in a different martial art style. As the translator explained my words, I could tell the sifu wasn't impressed with my background and had no clue what the words LimaLama even meant. He only said through the interpreter, "If you come here to learn, you learn."

I was told to put my hand up with the back of my wrist against his. This was the Ba Gua method for training or sparring. I was used to standing facing my opponent and bobbing and weaving, taking little steps forward and using all my weapons—hands, feet, knees, elbows. But the Ba Gua master said, "No," the interpreter explaining, "This is how we train."

We would walk in a circle, with our hand's palms facing out and pressed against our opponent's hand. It reminded me of the old Native American fighting tradition, where they tied a rope around your hand against your opponent's hand, then you would fight with knives until someone was dead. I thought to myself confidently, "I can do this. I'm ready."

So, as I stepped forward, *Pop*—I was on the ground. I jumped up and quickly said, "Do it again." We placed our hands up, palms out, against each other again; and as I began to move, Pow—I was on the floor. He never hit me with a fist or wrist slap. He hit me with what I can only describe as a snapping palm strike, almost like he had holes in his hands. I thought I could see his palm whip at impact. But he hit me so hard and fast, I couldn't see it coming.

The sifu was about my height, but he must have weighed barely 110 pounds, soaking wet. There was no way this guy should be knocking me down. His strikes were explosive; it felt like a sledgehammer hitting me, and I couldn't stop him. I wanted more of it. I wanted to learn to hit like him too. GM Tino hit the same way but only used his fingers to strike when we sparred. If he had used his hand, he could have hurt me. His size and strength were twice that of the Chinese sifu, but they both shared incredible striking power.

I kept getting up off the dirt floor, saying, "Do it again." He hit me so hard, but I liked it. I wanted to figure out what this sifu was doing. Before I knew it, *Bam!* He hit me so hard, I was almost knocked out. I was on the floor looking up. Pissed off, I jumped up and barked, "Come on!" I got in my usual fighting stance. He put his hand up again, and I said, "No, no, no, here!" I was in a fighting stance, ready to throw down. I wanted to fight him. But he shook his head and said, "No, here." He pointed with his palm up to meet mine.

So, we went at it again, and *Boom!* he swept my leg and I was on the floor again. He did it so easily. I didn't like the pain, but he did it so effortlessly. I wanted to fight. I said, "Come on, let's fight." And the interpreter said, "We are. This is how we spar." Ba Gua sparring was hard to figure out, and I wanted to learn it. I think he accepted me because I never quit; I kept getting up and getting knocked down. He knew I wanted to learn. He only charged me around $10 a month. He had between 15 to 20 students, which was good income in the Korean economy at that time. I was just happy to have found him and excited to learn a new martial art.

HONING THE SWORD

Ba Gua Quan Sifu.

I always tried to be there when the interpreter attended. If the interpreter wasn't around, Sifu would demonstrate a technique using another student. I'd motion for him to show me, and he'd oblige. I'd stand in the customary position with my wrist against his, moving slowly in a circle, until *Pow, pow, pow,* I'd get beat up. But I was already familiar with this kind of "hands on" training. This was how I learned LimaLama, with Master Sal kicking my ass at every training session.

After some time had passed and I was comfortable with my surroundings, I'd get to class early and tell the other students that Sifu had cancelled class for the day. I'd tell them, "Sifu isn't feeling good," or "Sifu had to go to Seoul today." They'd believe me and leave. I got about one month of private lessons with Sifu—until the students found out what I had been doing. It was October, so the students grabbed me and threw me in the river. It was frozen, and I got pneumonia as punishment. The students had taught me a hard lesson to not be selfish.

I would try to get information from advanced students; maybe one or two would show me a move, but most would say, "It's not your time yet." I was told that it takes 10 to 15 years to learn Ba Gua Quan. In fact, the internal arts of Ba Gua Quan, t'ai chi ch'uan and pinyin (gong fu) took a lifetime of learning.

Little by little, Sifu began introducing different Ba Gua movements, training preparation, and traditional methods for strengthening the body. I came to realize that this internal martial art was, as they say, "a moving meditation." Sifu also introduced me to darts, knives, and weapons. The training regime was both unique and tough. He would have us dig a hole about eight inches deep, and we would all be told to jump in and out of our manmade holes. The next time we'd dig our hole deeper, and the next time dig the hole even deeper, each time continuously jumping in and out of the hole. We were building discipline and leg strength.

There were holes all over the barn-dojo dirt floor that students had dug. The holes eventually got deep enough that it was like jumping onto a table. Another time, he used wooden stumps; he called it, "Holding up the Heavens." We'd have to stand in a horse position on the stumps. He'd light an incense and tell us to remain on the stump until the incense burned out. The thicker the incense, the longer it would burn. He told us, "Once you complete this exercise, I will teach you something different. We'd all be sweating; our legs would be shaking. He'd make us hold sticks and place weights on it to weigh us down even more. On reflection, I know today that he was teaching meditation, discipline, balance, and endurance through this exercise.

HONING THE SWORD

One time he was teaching me how to walk on a rope to improve my balance. I, the novice tightrope walker, fell off and got knocked out. I wore a neck brace for a month. I trained with him for about nine months. I wanted to stay in Korea to learn more, but I would be soon going back stateside to Fort Hood. What I learned from him would probably take another 10 years to master. His whipping palm technique was fast and fluid, but it hit you like a kicking mule. He didn't need any large swinging motion to effect his strike. I practiced it every day. It was similar to splashing hands in LimaLama. His skill and power were definitely at the same level of GM Tino, only packaged in a smaller body.

Ba Gua is an internal martial art. How you breathe and move is meditation for the mind and body. At the time of my training with Sifu, I was just too physical in my approach. I only wanted to fight. He wanted to teach me to use my mind better. But I only wanted to get good enough to be able to knock someone out faster. I realized, later in my life, that Ba Gua martial arts is best suited for older fighters. It required less action to get your intended result—to end the fight quickly.

I was just too young and hyped up for fighting. I wasn't ready to learn the meditative or spiritual side of the art. In Ba Gua training, the students would be walking and creating a circular trail on the dirt floor. All from the constant footwork. If they kicked you, it felt like a horse stepping on you. They'd step on your toes and, man, it would hurt for days. So, you constantly jump back and forth, training on footwork control. His was an "old school" way of teaching martial arts that I learned to admire and appreciate.

UNDERGROUND FIGHTS

During my tour of duty in Korea, I met a Coronel in the Korean Army. He was assigned to our base as liaison for the Korean

Army. I can't prove it, but I feel sure that the sifu taekwondo instructor on base informed the Korean Army colonel of my fight with the red belt sergeant at his dojo. Beating up an American was not an issue or concern to them. But disrespecting a Korean martial art may have been an incentive for the colonel to approach me and make a deal.

The colonel proposed to set up after-hour fights for money in the nearby villages. He could get me assigned as a photographer with him to ensure I'd have a gate pass. The fights occurred about once a month. I thought it was a great idea. I would get paid to fight and practice my techniques with other martial artists. I soon realized that whenever the Korean Army visited a village, they literally took over control of all aspects of the village economy and society.

My first fight was in a dingy-looking bar nightclub in a bad part of the village. The government frowned on unauthorized events that didn't use their facilities and/or pay a fee. But I was with the Korean colonel, who was free to roam about without being bothered. He told me that he was going to bet against me. He favored his own Korean countrymen and didn't want to see me beat them. I told him, "That's good. Because I bet on myself to win." Some fights would be held in large homes or areas where music could be loud, and a fight ring could be fabricated. At the clubs, the colonel's men would take control after closing time for regular customers, and only the people who paid to see and bet on the fights remained.

Think of the worst bar you've ever entered. The smoke, the smell of fermented stale fruit. Dirty, sticky tables and railings, and hard dirt floors. Trash all around. Dried squid, peanuts, and kimchee snacks all provided to make you thirsty for drinks. All the women were dancers or prostitutes. There were plenty of hardcore Korean homeboys from the village, all looking to make a name for themselves. The VIP crowd of gamblers sat in a special area overlooking the dance floor.

I fought in 8 to 10 underground fights during my tour of duty in Korea. Most matches were between and amongst Korean fighters, I was the lone outsider. All the fights ended when someone got hurt or was unable to continue. None of the fights ever lasted longer than two or three minutes. You either won, got knocked out, or were seriously injured. There was no such thing as a "draw" or judges' scorecard decision. Most fighters got knocked out from kicks to the head. The colonel always chose the best fighter from the village to fight me. My fights were usually the last fight. The coronel was determined to win his bet by finding worthy opponents to fight me.

One fight in particular was my toughest Korean street fight. We were in a nightclub. It was closed after midnight, so only the colonel, his friends, and people who had paid to watch the fights remained. For servicemen, there is a nightly curfew. After 12 midnight, you had to be on the base or at somebody's house. But since the colonel had gotten me the base gate pass, I wasn't worried about getting caught. There were about three or four fights before my match would begin. The colonel always saved me for the semi-main event or main event. On this night, I was the main event. I was wearing my black gi. I just took off my shoes, barefoot and ready to fight. These underground fights were incredibly fast. Somebody always went down from injury or knock out. I was always at the ready.

All the Korean fighters were strong. Their kicks were fast and powerful. If you weren't paying attention, you'd be "eating toes" and spitting teeth. In LimaLama, we did round kicks—sweeps to the leg. In taekwondo there are no kicks to the legs. They went to the head and body. But their kicks were incredibly swift and hard. On this night, the Korean fighter I battled was tall and lanky. I realized immediately that it was going to be hard to get inside his kicks, he had so much reach advantage. Sure enough, he drew first blood, busting my lip and nose. He also fractured one of my ribs with a side kick to the midsection. But it wasn't enough to stop me. I ended up hurting him.

When you're fighting a taekwondo opponent, you don't kick. They train to kick and defend against kicks. I did mix some kicks with my strikes; but against a kicker, you always use your hands. I would let him throw kicks and counter with punches to the body. I kicked his legs to stop his advance and moved forward, throwing combinations to the body. I finally hit him with a hook, and I ended up finishing him with a spinning back knuckle. The Korean fighters aren't used to that move. I almost caught him with an elbow, but he leaned back and so I used the back knuckle hammer. I knocked him out.

At first, the crowd was howling for him. Then they drew quiet when I dropped him. I loved it, raising my fists, and jumping around the room. I was my only fan at these underground fights, and I didn't care because I was getting paid. The colonel always lost money betting against me because I won all my fights. He called me his "Mexican Bandit," because he had to pay me to fight. Then I would take that all the money and place a bet for me to win. I robbed the colonel twice on every fight because I never lost. But I knew the colonel was making more money on his bets with the other fighters.

COMFORT CLERK

While serving in Korea, I was a mail clerk, then a supply clerk. Eventually, I was assigned as a health-and-comfort clerk at the military stockade. My job was to determine what the prisoners needed, such as toothpaste, soap, shampoo, paper, pencils, envelopes, etc. I would order it and then deliver the supplies to each prisoner. Their crimes were of no concern to me. I was just there to fulfill my duty as a soldier. In fact, I thought it was a good thing, having a clerk available to get them the supplies they wanted, or so I thought. Many would be talkative, enjoying the company of a clerk to pass the time; others rarely spoke a word.

There was a guy there doing time for murder and attempted murder. Supposedly, he had married a Korean woman. When it was time for him to go back to the states, his wife never showed up at the airport, and he had to leave. When he arrived at the Army base in the states, he figured out a way to get back to Korea. He went out looking for her and found her with another GI. He ended up stabbing the guy and killing him. He stabbed his wife too. Thinking her dead, he buried her, but she was still alive. She somehow managed to crawl out of her early grave and went to the police. He was arrested and turned over to the military police. He was in the stockade, waiting to be shipped back to the mainland to do his time.

I was delivering goods in the stockade when I went to his cell to give him his supplies. I recall he had never spoken to me but always had his supply list ready when I toured the cells. He was slightly taller than me and had a heavy build. He easily outweighed me by 25 pounds. As I was putting the supplies on the cell wall table, from the corner of my eye I saw him rushing forward to hit me. His fists were up and ready to punch me as he lunged. I immediately turned and hit him repeatedly. I cut his head open, breaking his jaw, ribs, and arm. I did a number on him. He never landed a punch. He lay unconscious in his own blood until medics and military patrol personnel arrived at the cell.

I had trained continuously for years, preparing for this kind of episode. I was always alert to my surroundings. Whether at school, the park, or neighborhood parties, I had trained to be ready to fight. I never looked for trouble, but I was always ready for it. If I saw a group of guys at a corner or in front of a building,

I knew there was always an idiot in the group. They might challenge me, asking "Where you from?" Instead of walking into that kind of situation, I would walk around it or avoid it completely. Some guys train and get paranoid, thinking trouble is around every corner. That is simply fear unrealized.

Most persons who have had experience and training, like military, law enforcement and security professionals, are always alert to their surroundings. It comes with the territory and is a learned behavior trait. This is the warrior mindset. Growing up in a tough neighborhood and attracting the attention of gang members reinforced my alertness. For gangbangers, if you're not with their gang, you are against them and become a target. I never feared altercations; on the contrary, if someone tried to accost me, I treated it as a free sparring opportunity. On the street, I just made sure to turn the corner a little wider to see what was coming my way. If someone tapped me on the shoulder, I didn't jump, I just looked back and moved over or turned around to see what they wanted.

This military stockade assignment was no different. Like any situation on the street, when someone tries to start a fight with me, I respond. Fortunately, I saw the punch coming and reacted immediately. I can't claim I used boxing, LimaLama, or any rudimentary Ba Gua skills to kick this murderer's butt. I was just instinctively fighting to defend myself. He must have thought he could take advantage of me while my back was turned. He was wrong. I don't know why he chose to attack me. It didn't matter. Because of his actions, he ended up getting hurt.

By this time in my life, I was highly trained for fighting. Fighting was a part of my psyche, my personality. Unfortunately for this prisoner, I knew to hit first, where to hit, and to keep hitting until the threat was stopped. The concept—LimaLama does not back up—wasn't just some training mantra for me. That is how I trained and how I fought. I never worried about blocking punches, because I would attack the punch and the body with unrelenting combinations. This usually meant there wouldn't be many punches coming back at me. That's how I approached my training, to be the best. I didn't give the prisoner in the stockade a chance. He never knew what hit him, until he woke up in a military hospital.

4
BECOMING A CHAMPION

BACK IN THE USA

MY TRAINING IN BA GUA was interrupted by the Army. I really wanted to stay in Korea and continue my training; instead, I was transferred back to the United States. When I arrived at Fort Hood, Texas, in early 1976, I was eventually assigned to the 256 MP Detachment. I had less than a year left to serve. When I arrived, the assignment clerks were looking at my background and saw that I had been assigned to military police (MP). The word got around that I was military police and couldn't be trusted. The guys in the barracks want to get high and do foolish stuff. I didn't care about any of that, but they thought I was an informant for the Army brass.

I got in some fights because of it. I told them, "If you want to fight, let's fight. I don't run from nobody." But they were stupid fights. These soldiers would be drinking and talking trash. When they were drunk enough to build up false bravado to fight, they got hurt. I made sure to put enough pain on their bodies that they would remember for weeks. As the unit got to know me, I would inform them that I was assigned to the stockade as a comfort clerk, not MP duties. They didn't believe me. I was looked on as an outcast, but it didn't matter to me.

I had never been a follower. After a few barracks, latrine, and parking-lot fights, I was moved to a different barracks.

I found out there was an open tournament on base. Black belts from all parts of Texas competed. I immediately signed up for the Katas and Black Belt competition. The judges initially were not going to let me perform because the color of my gi was black and because I refused to bow. All the other competitors wore white gi, so I really stood out among the fighters.

Since my LimaLama patch was displayed on my gi, I think they were inclined to just waive the gi color issue. I explained why LimaLama didn't bow during salutations, but I could see the judges were not happy. They then asked me to step back during my salutation. I told them, "No, LimaLama doesn't back up." I'm sure the judges thought I was too prideful or stubborn, but I didn't think so. The LimaLama salutation had special meaning to me. I felt it was disrespectful of the judges to ask me to change it. I realized by my actions; I had the put the judges against me. They probably thought I was rebellious, going against their rules on the tournament. After some discussion, the judges relented and allowed me to wear my gi and ignored my salutation.

Most of the competitors had martial arts backgrounds in karate. I noticed that the Kata competitors were using hard, power-form methods with their punches and kicks. I decided I would integrate LimaLama's fluid wrist slaps, and Ba Gua palm and low-stance techniques to stand out from the others. This was a risk, since the judges, most of them karate black belts, may not have considered my Kata style to be equal to the precision and power-packed moves of the other karate competitors.

I won Grand Champion in Kata competition and got a standing ovation from the audience. When the black belt competitions began, I won my five preliminary bouts and made it to the championship round. I fought a six-ranked martial artist in the black belt division from Santa Maria, Texas. I thought I had won the fight—just like most fighters do—but he was awarded the win. I received a loud standing ovation when they announced my name. When they announced him as the winner of the tournament, the crowd booed him. It just so happened that he was the brother of the tournament promoter.

That happens often in local tournaments, so I was not surprised. People favor their local guy. It didn't matter to me; I knew I had represented LimaLama well on the mat. After the tournament, he came up to me and told me, *"You beat me."* He offered me the trophy, but I told him, *"I don't need another trophy. I have hundreds of them collecting dust at home in California."* I was surrounded by many people asking about my martial art style. None had ever heard of LimaLama. I was invited by some local black belts to visit their dojos; I took them up on their offers. I was always proud to share my LimaLama history with other martial artists and the curious people I met at tournaments.

During my stay at Fort Hood, I tried out and was assigned to the Army boxing team. I joined the team to be able to continue my fight training regime and avoid guard duty. I only had three months left to serve, and it turned out to be beneficial. I fought in four amateur boxing matches at 122 or 126 pounds. I won all my boxing matches. I also represented the Army in at least, 18 martial arts tournaments in Texas and Oklahoma.

In Austin, Texas, I met this rich guy who offered to sponsor me in the tournaments. He liked me and the way I fought. I gladly accepted because it meant I could fight people outside Texas and the local area. He would fly me to different tournaments; and in return, I trained him for about six or seven months in LimaLama during my stay at Fort Hood. I won most of the tournaments he sponsored me for. As usual, the ones I lost were because of disqualification for excessive contact or drawing of blood.

If there were any form competitions, I blended Ba Gua in my forms technique to spice it up. I fought one time in the Championship round in Oklahoma. The guy was a good fighter, but I think I had gotten the advantage from the start. I did an axe kick, hitting my opponent so hard I pulled a muscle in my butt. I used the axe kick because most of my opponents didn't expect it from a LimaLama-trained fighter.

LimaLama is 80 percent hands and 20 percent kicks. The judges thought about disqualifying me but didn't. They gave him the points for my hard hit. My butt hurt bad every time I moved, but I went on fighting, trying not to let my opponent know. It was a good fight. He ultimately won the fight on points, but I came in second place in the overall tournament. My butt hurt for a few months thereafter until the muscle and nerve finally relaxed. It didn't matter; I continued to train daily, despite the pain.

Specialist, 1st Class, Lorenzo Rodriguez, 1977.

The Army tried to have me re-up for four more years. I wanted to stay but only if they would keep me in special services so I could train and fight in tournaments representing the Army. They said no, so my time in the military was finally coming to an end. I told the Army I lived in Hawaii, so I could have a vacation before going home. One of the guys in my platoon gave me his family address in Hawaii to use for departure. That gave me a free ride from the Army to Hawaii.

THE CALIFORNIA KID

I spent a week or so in Hawaii to wind down from the service experience and relax. When I returned home to California, I stayed at my family home in El Monte. I hadn't told anyone in the martial arts community that I had returned home. I was busy cleaning the backyard one morning when my neighbor stopped by and mentioned an Open LimaLama karate tournament being held at Rosemead High School that day. So, I immediately grabbed my gi and got to the high school with enough time to compete in the black belt competition. This open competition had no weight or height restrictions. I would be fighting the *best of the best* that day. In the past, Master Sal would have tournaments there, because that's the school his sons had attended. I found out later in the day that this event was sponsored by Master Sal. But he didn't know that I had entered the competition until the final round.

On hindsight, what motivated me to hurry down to the tournament was a subconscious need to see if I still had the drive for fighting at the level I had before, and to see what the competition looked like since my absence from California. Most tournaments start with the young kids in Katas and sparring competitions. When I got there, the tournament had just begun the brown belt division fights. I had missed the adult Kata competition. I didn't mind; I was just glad to be there to fight.

Nobody recognized me. So, the competition probably thought I'd be an easy draw. None of my fights were ever easy in tournaments. I always assumed my opponent was like me, looking to knock my head off. So, I was always ready for war in the ring or mat. Even if I won, I never took an opponent for granted. When I was on the mat, I meant to attack my opponent, and I expected to be attacked as well. This had been my LimaLama training mindset since I began in martial arts. This tournament would be no different.

The competitors saw my salutation to the judges and recognized the LimaLama patch on my gi. Many tournaments required that we bow to the judges and opponent. But LimaLama doesn't bow. But I was now in southern California, and the judges were aware of the LimaLama salutation tradition GM Tino had established and said nothing. However, the Japanese and Korean judges with martial arts backgrounds always wanted you to bow out of respect of the arts but I wouldn't do it. So, as usual, I was already cutting against the grain of traditional martial arts rituals.

A lot of fighters would go to small local tournaments to stay physically sharp and to build their rating. On this day, I had won my first four fights. I used angles, always moving forward to score points, but I ended up going toe to toe with every opponent that day. Everyone came determined to win. I loved it! I eventually made it to the championship round.

My opponent for the tournament championship was a guy named Steve Fisher. He had studied Shōrin-Ryū Karate under the watchful eyes of international champions Tadashi Yamashita and Mike Stone. Years later, he would earn his 7th degree black belt. He was known as "The California Kid." He was a good fighter. Steve was respected in the local martial arts community. At the time, he had been winning all the tournaments, so he was the favorite in this tournament too. I always looked forward to fighting someone with a reputation. Because if I won, I would be expanding LimaLama's reputation.

We were the last two competitors to fight in the tournament. Four judges surrounded the square mat, and one referee was on the mat. We fought for two minutes. First one to score three points would win the bout and the tournament championship. Every time I fought in the street or in tournaments, I used combinations. I would be attacking the opponent. I never used singular strikes for points. But, in karate tournaments, you can only receive a point for a strike that was confirmed by the judges. When the other judges see a punch or elbow or kick, they raise a flag. The referee would ask, "What did you see?" If there is no agreement among the judges to confirm the point, I wouldn't get the point. I would argue with the referee that it shouldn't matter where I hit him; I should get the point. That usually made the referee dislike me for disagreeing with him. I didn't care; I had no problem pushing back on "no calls" from judges. It was my fight, and they were denying me my points.

Steve would move in a circle. It looked like a cockfight. Point-tournaments force you to look for an opening to strike and earn a point. If you got close to the head—without contact—you could earn a point. In my view, if you are going to the head, then hit it! We traded kicks and combinations. I quickly recognized that he had a good reverse punch. At one point, I hit him in the ribs and swept him, dropping him to the floor. The judges had to score the point for me. When we resumed fighting, he faked a kick and instead threw a back knuckle on the side of my head. He had rung my ear but wasn't disqualified. I don't know why the judges failed to call the foul. I can only guess, maybe because he was well known and was liked by the tournament people. It didn't matter, no action was taken. The score was tied 2-2.

There was still time left. The next point scored would win. Every time you leave the mat you are given a warning. I had run Steve off the mat twice. He was warned both times by the referee. I faked like I was going to go after him and stopped. He was backing up and attempted a high kick. I dropped to the mat and kicked him in the groin. It was a drop kick. The audience went nuts, applauding my technique. Steve acted like I had gone too hard. The kick wasn't allowed as a point because the judges couldn't confirm if I had kicked too hard. So, they gave him a few minutes to recover. The fight was now going into overtime.

Steve and I immediately went at it again. We both wanted to take the advantage. We simultaneously moved forward with combinations, striking each other. But no judge raised their flags to give either of us a point. I didn't care anymore because now we were just fighting. Steve attempted a back knuckle, which I thought was too far away from my face. They gave him a point for the attempted strike. If he had hit me, I wouldn't have complained about it.

I went after him, but the referee stopped the fight. It may have looked like I was retaliating or being a bad sport for losing, but at that moment I didn't think he scored a point. They ended up giving Steve the match, and he won the tournament. I can only imagine that the spectators and tournament people, having been there all day, wanted to go home. So, the long day might have influenced the decision for the judges to give him the point and get the tournament finished. That's the thing about fighters, and I was no different: If we aren't hurt or knocked out, we always believe we won the fight.

I was pissed off, so naturally, I approached Steve and told him. "If you're going to hit me with that back knuckle, then hit me. It was too far from my face for you to have earned the point. If you did that on the street, it wouldn't have done anything."

Steve responded, "Hey, that's the way the game is played. Who are you?"

I told him, "Lorenzo Rodriguez."

He looked me in the eye. "Man, you gave me a beating. If you hadn't fought me, you would have won first place."

"Yeah, whatever. You know who won today."

When they announced the first, second, and third place winners for the black belt championship, I got on the podium with Steve and turned to him. "You know who won. You know I beat you."

Steve looked at me and winked, raising his thumb to acknowledge my statement and saying, "If you want the trophy, we can exchange."

I told him, "No, let them announce that I won." Steve just smiled at me and quickly left the podium. He knew I had won the fight. Over time, I would see him at different karate tournaments. We never did get to fight again, but remained cordial.

SAL ESQUIVEL'S LIMALAMA INCORPORATED

I had been training in my parents' backyard, but that came with many limitations. I had no one to train with, or equipment to use. I also went to the South El Monte Parks and Recreation Center to work out. But I was limited in the time I could use the facilities because of all the programs they had going on. People would often approach me to see what I was doing and asked questions about training that interrupted my training regime. I didn't really want to go back to the schools I had been at before. Master Sal never opened his own school. He used facilities and paid a portion of his profits to use locations without the burden of any overhead. Financially, it probably made a lot of sense. But he had kept me and other black belts on the hook because he would also talk about opening a commercial martial arts school. It never happened.

What he did have was some of the best fighters in the area. Some of Master Sal's students eventually opened their own studio and had paid Master Sal a fee as Grandmaster for the school. He would be paid to provide training to the black belts and brown belts and a fee for judging promotions to black belt at his former students dojos.

My father owned some buildings in the El Monte Valley Mall. One location was perfect for opening a school. Parking was bad, but it had plenty of open space for me to train and teach large classes. I got a lot of interest from people walking by and asking if I would be opening a gym. I asked Danny if he wanted to go into partnership on a commercial school. He agreed, and we opened the Sal Esquivel LimaLama Incorporated school in early 1979. I was only a 1st degree black belt and still had not received my certificate from Master Sal. Master Sal claimed that according to the LimaLama Organization bylaws, only a 3rd degree black belt could open a LimaLama school. But with his son, Danny, as my partner, he never voiced any concerns. Danny and I had the school for almost a year.

I ran into trouble with other neighboring businesses not long after opening our school. There was a bar on one side and nightclub on the other side of our school. Parking for our school was limited because it was closed in. You could only back your car out of the parking spot in order to leave. There were only a few parking spots located in front of our front door. On Saturdays, there was always a large crowd at the nightclub, and they would always block our cars. I had to go to the bar and nightclub and tell the DJ and the band members, "Hey, I'm blocked in. You need to move your cars so I can get out. If you don't, I going to have the cars towed away." This happened a lot, and I got tired of having to remind the bar and club management about it. There was a sign clearly posted that illegal parking was subject to being towed away. So, I started calling the police department to have those cars towed away.

Sure enough, every Monday, guys showed up at my school threatening me and saying I owed them for having to pay the fine for getting towed. Most of the time they'd whine about it and leave. I'd tell them, "There's a big sign outside that says your car will be towed if you are blocking the cars parked here. But you still block me in. I'm not paying for shit." Sometimes my morning classes would be going on when these assholes walked in, interrupting the class.

I remember one guy threatened me: "I know martial arts, and if you don't pay me, I'm going to kick your ass." I immediately told my students, "Get the hell out! Go through the back door." I then walked over and locked the front door and turned my attention to the idiot who had just challenged me. He said he was a martial artist, so I didn't give him any chance to prove it. I walked up and started hitting him; he never had a chance to throw a punch. He'd try to get up, and I'd knock him down again. This scene happened a few times with different guys throughout the period I had the school at the Valley Mall. I called them my "car tow" fights—a free workout on human dummies for me to pound to the ground for free.

On reflection, it was kind of dumb for me to assault these intruders, considering I was a black belt, and I was the one who always hit first. I could have been arrested or sued if they had been injured. At the time, my mindset was they had come to my place and threatened me, so they got what they deserved. But they also could have escalated the problem by coming back with more dudes, waiting for me after closing time. Or worse, they could come and shoot up the place. They all knew where I was located. It was like high school all over again. But I was still young and thought I was invincible. I wasn't invincible, I was lucky.

We had a good school with over 40 students participating regularly. Master Sal would come in about once a month to give a seminar in LimaLama. He and Danny had one of those father/son relationships where they didn't get along. Master Sal would show up and demonstrate a technique and then change the technique. He did that a lot. It would anger Danny, who would say to him, "How are we to teach students a technique and then you change it 10 minutes later? And then change it again to something different moments later?" GM Tino would do the same thing. Danny would begin arguing about the changes with his father. In the meantime, I would be practicing all three variations of the technique. I would tell Danny, "Stop arguing with your dad. Just call this move "A," this one, "B," and this one "C." Danny, frustrated, would point out that Master Sal always did that. And I would remind him, "That's the way he is. You're not going to change him, so let it go."

After nearly a year of running the school, I injured my knee playing sand volleyball at Puddingstone Park. I had torn cartilage, requiring me to wear a cast on my right knee. Fortunately, the cast was perfect for kicking. The cast had a rubber ball at the bottom. I wasn't able to train with our students for about three months. I didn't want to train kids because it didn't look good for me to be in a cast and on medication at the school. I was out of the school for nearly two months, only stopping by early or late in the day to manage the business paperwork.

Danny was married with a family and was not always available to teach. He was a strict instructor who could work well with the high-school-age students and adults. With younger students, it seemed he never had the patience to allow them to enjoy the training. We were losing students, and I wasn't sure what was happening at the school.

I asked my sister to take me to the school one day during the children's class. Danny was teaching. It was obvious, watching his teaching style, that he was too strict and impatient with the kids. I saw him interacting with this one little boy. He was tough on him, almost abusive. The parents didn't say anything, but they looked unhappy. I was unhappy too. I decided then that something had to be done. I left and went straight to the bank and pulled all the money out from our account. I went back to the school and, after all the students left, Danny and I had a heart-to-heart talk.

I began, "Danny, I saw how you taught the class. I don't like the way you teach the kids. You are too hard on them. And I know you can't change your teaching style. The bottom line is that we've lost too many of our students since I've been away. We have a choice. One of us has to leave."

Danny nodded in agreement. I realized that if I left the business, he could be sure that my father would have him vacate the facility. If he left the business, maybe the school could survive. I offered to give him half the bank account balance that day. What I should have added was, "After we pay the outstanding bills." Danny agreed and took his share.

Master Sal came by a week later, after I was on my own running the school. He wanted me to sign a franchise contract that I would be under him until I was a 3rd degree black belt. There would be a fee charged for it and a separate fee for the monthly seminar appearances. He didn't do that when Danny was a partner because it would be taking money out of his son's pocket. I couldn't afford his offer because I was just starting over again. I knew he would just keep me stringing along for years to reach the 3rd-degree level. Besides, he had yet to give me my certificate as a black belt. I declined his offer.

He eventually sent one of his black belt goons, a guy named David Velazquez. David had arrived in his LimaLama gi. I knew it was intended to be a challenge. I walked up to him, looking at his uniform. "What is this?"

He told me, "Sal said you have to take the 'LimaLama Incorporated' sign down or sign the contract. You can't teach LimaLama until you've reached your 3rd degree."

I looked at him and said, "Shit. First, it took this long to get promoted and get to this level. How long will it take for me to get my 3rd degree? Second, why would I stay with an organization that is not helping me? Instead, he is trying to blackmail me in order to keep my school. Third, Sal sends idiots like you to try and threaten me."

David said nothing, so I continued, "I won't benefit if I kick your ass. Go ahead, take the sign down. He painted it. He created it. The bottom line is I'm going to teach what I teach. I'm gonna teach LimaLama because that is all I know. I might call it something else, but I am going to teach."

I walked over and grabbed the paper banner hanging on the front window and tore it down. I crumpled it up and threw it on the ground in front of him.

David picked up the banner. "You're being blackballed. You can't call it LimaLama."

I told him, "Well, that's life. I don't care. I'm going to continue my school."

A part of me hoped he'd try to fight, but I knew he really didn't want to test my resolve. He made the right decision to walk out of my school.

EL MONTE SELF DEFENSE SCHOOL

I kept my school doors open after David left. I wasn't concerned about the veiled threats or some goon black belt of Sal's trying to intimidate me. Eventually I increased student membership. My students were doing well in tournaments and getting noticed. The LimaLama belt structure was white, purple, blue, green, brown, and black. When I first started in LimaLama, there was only white, brown, and black. The other belts were added later by Master Sal and Master Richard. Years later, as the school instructor, I added yellow and orange belts because there was too much to learn between white and purple. Besides, students were motivated to continue to progress when they moved up a belt.

A few weeks after my encounter with David, Master Sal showed up at the school and wanted to speak with the kids' class. I still respected him as a master and allowed him to speak. I introduced him as my first instructor and gave the parents and teachers some background on his history. It was a mistake. He tried to belittle me, telling the class that I wasn't a black belt (I was but he withheld my certificate because I refused to follow the dumb tradition of other black belts hitting me). He told the audience that what I was teaching wasn't LimaLama.

History always seems to repeat itself. Sal's master, GM Dan Guzman, had tried to shame him too when Sal left the Kenpo organization, years before, to be under GM Tino. So here he was now trying to belittle me in the same fashion his master had done with him. Master Sal looked at me and said, "You need me, or else you can't continue to teach."

I told him, "No I don't!" I immediately took off my belt and dropped it on the floor. "I don't need that belt. I'm still going to teach the same. I'm going to teach what I know. I've been representing LimaLama forever. Wherever I have gone, I've represented LimaLama. All I know is LimaLama. Even if I change the name of the school, I will be teaching LimaLama."

Thankfully, many parents spoke out: "Who's this man?"

I told them, "He was my first instructor."

The parents continued to shout, "We don't care who he is. We like what you're doing with our kids." The parents ended up praising me and telling him to leave.

Master Sal left, but only after calling my school a fraud. I was taken completely off guard by Master Sal, as I am sure the parents of my students were too. Master Sal had tried to dishonor me and my school. Thankfully, parents told me, "We like what you do with our kids. We like that they're doing better in school. We like that our kids are showing respect. We like going to the tournaments with you and seeing our kids show confidence. They take care of themselves. The change in them has been great. We will stay with you as long as your gym is open." Instead of Master Sal publicly shaming me, making me quit my school or begging his forgiveness; I ended up with the parents praising me for all I had done with their children. I felt vindicated by the best court, the Court of Public Opinion.

About a month later, Master Sal came back to the school in the evening. He wanted to provoke me to fight with him. At the time, I had just started getting into the kickboxing tournaments and was in great fighting shape. I told him, "I'm no dummy. I've been in the service, and I know I can't challenge someone higher ranked than me, physically. Instead, I'll beat you up on paper. By documenting the threat. I'm not a kid anymore. Go ahead, take your best shot. Hit me! I'll be driving your Cadillac and living in your house. Years ago, I would have gone toe to toe with you, and you probably would have kicked my ass. But not today. I'm not a kid anymore.

"Instead of fighting you, I'll call my lawyer and sue you. You already have a record for assaults, and you've been doing martial arts all your life. I've got witnesses. Look at all the people outside this window. You came to *my* school to threaten me. I don't need to fight you now; I'm smarter than that." I had caught him completely off guard.

He probably thought he could still kick my ass or worse, have me shaking in fear. Instead, I had used verbal judo and had him off balance from the moment he came in the building. Whatever he had thought about doing, he now thought twice and realized he could ultimately lose more than he bargained on. Before he walked out, Master Sal told me that I was no longer part of the LimaLama family and could not use the LimaLama patch. He said, GM Tino was made aware of what had occurred and that I was permanently blackballed from LimaLama.

Aerial view of El Monte Self Defense School, circa, 1979.

I knew I would have to find a way to promote my students without Master Sal's involvement. I changed our gi colors to black pants with a white top. I put a circle and around it, on the left side front of the top, "El Monte Self Defense School." In the middle of the back, I put a dragon on it. Underneath one arm I put a patch with the initials "LL," and underneath the other arm, a patch, in Japanese writing, that said, "Karate." I was determined to have the best school in the region. The best payback for being blackballed from Master Sal's school was to have El Monte Self Defense School be successful in tournaments. That became my goal, and I soon achieved it.

ARK WONG'S SCHOOL

It was mid-1980. I had been unsuccessful in contacting GM Tino. I recalled he and other masters had trained with Ark Wong at his school in China Town, so I thought I'd investigate and see why Tino had attended the kung fu school. I made an appointment to meet with Grandmaster Wong. At this stage of his life, he was more involved in the medicinal side of the arts. He interviewed me and wanted to know what background I had and why I wanted to join his school. He didn't seem impressed but accepted me as a student.

I was assigned outside, in the back of the school. All beginners began their kung fu training there. His student teachers ran drills and basic stance and form exercises. I mastered the forms quickly, only because of my previous training as a black belt. I continued about six months. I was tested on basic forms and movements. I passed them easily.

The school had patterns on the floor, and we were to follow the patterns in our drills. A horse stance, guard, movement, and side stances. They were what I'd call *old school* training. They had gung fu stances, real wide and low positions. They were trying to build up leg strength and stamina, the foundation for all martial arts. We didn't spar. Basically, it was only conditioning with some basic routines. As a black belt, I understood why the training regime was done and the benefit for it. Partly it was an initiation: can you handle the pressure and the drills? New students had to bear the discomfort of training, not really understanding what the drills meant. I would return to my school and practice all the forms before my students arrived for their classes in kickboxing or LimaLama.

GM Wong had half barrels in the back. Each had sand, pebble, powder, and smooth round marble shapes. We were to punch or spear these to build strength in our hands and fingers. I think a lot of the routines were testing us to see if we were committed to continue learning. If it was hot or cold out, it didn't matter, we trained. The only time we didn't train was if it was raining. They did a drill that reminded me of my Ba Gua master in Korea. We'd be in a horse stance with our arms raised to our sides and rings placed on our wrists. We'd had to hold the position until they told us to stop. Or we'd hold buckets of water running up and down stairs. It was merely *pain* initiation. Pain was something I had already become accustomed to in LimaLama training.

After about six months, I was finally moved inside. There, Wong's instructors taught basic forms and weapons. I think the form was called the "Flower" or "Plum." They'd teach a technique where one guy would punch, and another guy would defend himself. That was pretty much it. I don't recall any real sparring. I figured the instructors didn't want anyone to get hurt. They wanted to improve the strength and mental stamina of students. Those who continued to train would test; and if they passed, they would be introduced to a new technique.

I stopped training at GM Wong's school after a year had passed. I was training more students at my school and still competing in kickboxing tournaments. I had also started working full time in pest control in the early morning and teaching at my school right after work. I didn't have time to train in Sil Lum kung fu and didn't feel my time at the Wong School had improved my fighting skill. If I had remained, perhaps the training would have advanced. I can't honestly say that I learned anything new. Regardless, my original intent was to find out why GM Tino had gone to learn under GM Wong and also to add the experience to my résumé.

I figured that I could learn something to make my fighting stronger. It doesn't always happen. Sometimes the trainer makes the fighter better. Sometimes the fighter is already good, and the trainer doesn't provide anything to improve his skills. If I had stayed with GM Wong, maybe I would have improved. Most of the techniques are connectors to the next set of forms. Some are useful, some are discarded for the next technique. The loyal student is told which technique is more effective, and they remain to learn more. Presumably, they remain loyal to that art. I was already a black belt and loyal to my art form because it worked. It may be that the Wong Instructors felt I was not loyal to their martial art style, so no effort was made to advance my training. For that reason and my other obligations, I wasn't inclined to remain a student of Sil Lum.

THUMPER

My students would compete about once a month in local tournaments. I trained them as I had been trained, to move forward with combinations, always attacking. If my students competed, then I competed too. The students and I participated in the Kata (form) competition and belt competitions. My students all did well, and soon my school was becoming more popular in the area.

I competed to show my students that I was still young enough to be an active competitor too. I could still bang with the best martial artists. My students were like me in tournaments. If they didn't win, they got disqualified. The students saw me win at tournaments. They gave me the nickname "Thumper." I thought it was because I had the habit of saying right before the tournament began, "Okay, it's thumping time. It's time to cha-cha." But it wasn't. The students noticed my feet

BECOMING A CHAMPION

move like a rabbit in competition. I was always moving my feet like a dance step to distract my opponent. So, in tournaments, I was called Lorenzo "Thumper" Rodriguez. My students gave me a little rabbit doll dressed up in our gi colors and patches with "Thumper Rodriguez" on the back. It was pretty cool.

I didn't want my students to "politic" at the tournaments, shaking hands with judges, talking, or cozying up to tournament sponsors. We were a small school, but we were aggressive; we didn't need to kiss up to judges and sponsors. My students went to fight, and they fought tough. I'd always remind my kids—as I reminded myself too, "Fight hard, but just don't hit your opponent in the face." After a while, our school gi began getting recognized. Other martial artists would visit my school to spar, and some joined. I always wore the LimaLama patch on my gi when I competed in tournaments. Likewise, I continued to use and teach my students the LimaLama salutation that I had been taught by Master Sal. Even though our school's name had changed, the training remained the same LimaLama principles I had been taught. Our competitors certainly knew they were fighting LimaLama martial artists.

Some of the students wanted to do forms (Katas). I would work with them to see what they were good at. I had realized over the years that Kata training was harder to learn than sparring or tournament competitions, because you had only yourself to compete against. If you messed up, it was your fault. When I first started training in martial arts, Katas seemed like dancing to me. I didn't want to dance, I wanted to fight. But I soon realized that Kata training forced you to concentrate on all your movements, like a dancer would do.

You had to focus and master all the combination techniques and foot movements. As I matured, I always studied the judges; if their background was in taekwondo, I would make sure that my form kicks were sharp. If it was a Kempo judge, the punching combinations had to be fast and strong. I tried to give the judges what they liked or what they were familiar with. As much as I had been disappointed by Master Sal and all the bullshit about my black belt status, I must give him credit for my success in Kata competitions. Kata training was one of the things he demanded of me. He forced me to enter Kata competitions where, if given a choice, I would have avoided them completely. Because of him, I prospered in my techniques and my students prospered in their training and competitions.

THE IKBA CIRCUIT

I would have fought in many if not all the major and local tournaments I knew of during my fighting days, but it cost money to attend. I could afford to compete in most of the local or regional tournaments, but the bigger tournaments could cost hundreds of dollars to cover admission, hotel room, and meals. At that time, it was a lot of money. I simply couldn't afford it and have money left to support my martial arts school and family. Besides, spending all that money and only getting a trophy—it wasn't worth it. But I always wanted to go. I didn't have the experience of a trainer or promoter at that time. I didn't know how to approach promoters, and I couldn't write a proposal. I was just a fighter; it was all I knew. If there was a championship belt on the line, I tried to find a way to compete. But it didn't happen often enough for me. Life gives us challenges that we don't see coming most of the time.

In the early 1970s, when kickboxing first came to California, it was pretty wild. None of the fighters knew what the rules were because they were changing all the time. Every tournament was different. Promoters didn't want boxers to dominate fights, so minimum kicks per round were added. Also, we would use our karate gloves for kickboxing fights. It would be a few years before padding was introduced.

BECOMING A CHAMPION

In the summer of 1981, there was a kickboxing show at the Pico Rivera Sports Auditorium that was sponsored by the International Kickboxing Association (IKBA), with Danny Rodarte as promoter. Benny "The Jet" Urquidez had taken a team to compete. Ruben, his brother-in-law, was working the corner. I had attended with some students from my school and realized that kickboxing was much like the full-contact karate that I had been involved with in Texas.

Danny Rodarte had started training in Kenpo Karate with Ed Parker in 1964. He eventually received his 1st degree black belt in 1969. In 1980, Danny had made his 5th degree black belt, and during that same period he started to promote muay Thai fights under the IKBA he had helped promote. There was a scheduled IKBA tournament at the Culver City Auditorium in a few months, and I decided to take a team and try it out.

I began training my students like they were gladiators. I had no idea how to prepare for kickboxing fights, but I knew conditioning was crucial. I started them with three- to four-mile runs every day before they even started training in the gym. I tripled the kicking regime of front and side kicks to tax their legs. I started with 35 students and ended up with one, me.

If it weren't for the LimaLama classes that they all were enrolled in, I would have had to close down the school. I realized I had to mellow out and pare down my expectations. I had been overworking them. I contacted Danny, and he agreed to promote my fight in the upcoming tournament.

My first kickboxing fight turned out to be for the IKBA California Lightweight Champion title against a guy named Mark "Irish" Ives. He was of Mexican and Irish decent—a volatile blood mix—which made him more dangerous as a fighter, from my point of view. He trained under Frank Trejo, another Kenpo black belt from Ed Parker's school. Frank was a great trainer.

Mark had fought in kickboxing before this fight for the title. He had already held the Junior Lightweight title at the time I fought him. He was going for his second title belt. The California Lightweight belt (135 pounds) was vacant. Danny Rodarte was his promoter. There were quite a few competitors at the tournament. The California State Athletic Commission had sanctioned the fights.

I had sold a large number of tickets for the tournament. It was understood that a portion of the ticket sales would be given back to the fighters as "training expenses." Danny came over to me and said, "Look, your opponent didn't show up. You're here, and we have this other guy here, Mark Ives. You can fight him for the vacant title."

I looked at him and said, "That guy has experience and a title. This is my first time. Sure, I'll fight anyone for a title, but you're gonna have to pay me more." I wasn't surprised that competitors didn't show up to fight. That happened often in karate tournaments. Guys would get their name and picture on the schedule and wouldn't show up to fight. Many of them would try to pick and choose who they would fight at the last minute to protect their image and ranking. But the truth was, I didn't care; I just wanted to fight. If my opponent was ranked or a champion, that was even better. Danny agreed to pay me more money and give me a percentage of the tickets I had already sold for the tournament. Suddenly I was fighting for a title in my first kickboxing match. I suspected Danny figured I'd be an easy win for his fighter. I was out to prove him wrong.

Robert Alcazar had been training me. His expertise was in boxing, but for this fight I was using more kicks. It was a five-round fight. I believe Robert figured that a five-round fight couldn't be difficult compared to the 10- to 12-round fights for boxers. So, he keyed on my boxing skills more than conditioning for the bout. During the fight, I realized my conditioning was not good. I had not run enough to build stamina for the fight. We were training on carpets. It is a big difference from a ring where the padding, mat, and ropes can take energy from you.

Mark Ives and I went at it at the first bell. He was a good fighter. By the third round, I was out of gas. I was in the corner thinking, *Oh shit, I still have two rounds to go*. When the fourth round started. Mark and I went toe to toe. We went at it. It was a good fight. He had great leg kicks and had a reach advantage. I gained an advantage by staying inside him. I was more aggressive. Finally, I got my second wind. I dropped him twice in the fight, but in the end, they called it a draw.

Mark Ives and the promoter, Robert Alcazar, had both trained under Ed Parker and Kenpo. Most of the judges and competitors were from Kenpo Karate. It isn't rocket science to figure out that the judges would be partial to Kenpo fighters. I failed to realize, until after the decision, that the only way to be sure I'd get a win was to knock out my opponent. I didn't agree with the decision of the judges, but as a fighter, of course we always think we won any fight called a draw.

Mark Ives had more fights than I did in kickboxing and was already holding the IKBA Junior Lightweight Kickboxing title, so he should have dominated our fight. He was a great fighter, and his kicks were fast and powerful. But this was my first kickboxing match, and it was a title fight. I had trained hard, but probably not wisely. Regardless, I felt I had represented myself and LimaLama well. I was stronger and faster with my punches but couldn't get the winning call. In hindsight, getting a draw in my first ever kickboxing match should be considered a good outcome. But in my youthful mind, it was the same as losing. And I never took losing very well.

The following month we were supposed to do the rematch. I trained harder for this bout, with more focus on my conditioning. I was determined not to run out of gas this time around. We drove to Culver City, and instead of a crowd of martial arts fans and competitors, we found a three by five card on the arena door saying, "*Show cancelled until further notice.*" I was pissed off and angry. Pinché Danny Rodarte didn't even have the courtesy or "huevos" to call me to tell me the fight was cancelled. Instead, I had to drive out to Culver City to find out the truth on a three by five card! I had sold a large number of tickets for this match. The cancellation gave me more fuel for fire, and I trained even harder.

I really couldn't say anything to Rodarte about canceling the tournament and failing to inform me ahead of the match. He was the promoter, but his actions were unprofessional. If I had called him out, then I would have been the one who was unprofessional, and he would have removed me from future competitions. I wanted to fight, so I decided to take out my frustration on his fighter.

The following month, Mark and I had the rematch at the Culver City Auditorium. There were a lot of fights on the card. We were the semi-main event. I believe Danny "Magic" Lopez fought on the main card as a middleweight. I felt I had gone the distance in the last fight with Mark but wasn't given any respect from Rodarte to get a call about it. I fully intended to take out my frustrations on Mark and kick his ass this time. When I got there, I weighed in, but Mark didn't show up for the weigh-in. I was told he had already weighed in. I spoke up immediately. "No, no. We both need to weigh in together. It's not fair." The officials had to find Mark and bring him back to weigh in. He weighed a few pounds over the 135-pound limit. I wanted the fight, so we moved forward, retiring to our lockers to glove up.

When I entered the ring for our bout, I saw that my gloves were a different color from Mark's gloves. We soon realized that his corner gave him 8-ounce red gloves and we got 12-ounce blue ones. Once again, I spoke up. "We both get the same color and weight size gloves, or I don't fight." They claimed it was a mistake and didn't realize it. That was all bullshit. They were trying to give him an advantage. In the ring, they finally exchanged the gloves, the referee checked them both, and we strapped them up so we could get the fight started. If my blood wasn't pumping before, for sure it was boiling now. The draw, the bout cancellation, the weigh-in, and the gloves. That was all bullshit. If Mark wanted a fair fight, he shouldn't have allowed those things to happen. There was a simple solution: "You want to win, then kick my ass!"

They announced me as Lorenzo "Thumper" Rodriguez and Mark as the IKBA Lightweight Champion. The bell rang for the first round, and I had to chase Mark around the ring. In the second round, Mark didn't want to come out of his corner, but Frank Trejo pushed him out, telling him, "You got to fight!" I was aggressive; I went after him. Instead of calming down and picking my shots, I just wanted to kick his ass. Mark finally decided to fight and caught me a few times to the body and head, but I shook it off. It didn't do anything to slow me down. I still went after him, striking and kicking him repeatedly. I focused on his hips, knowing that he would lose balance from repeated kicks to the hip and legs.

The fight went the full five rounds. I won by unanimous decision. I was shadow boxing in the ring and saw Danny Rodarte sitting ringside. I raised my leg and stuck it out toward him, like I was aiming the kick at his head. I realized then that he was sitting in a wheelchair. I found out later that he had been in Thailand the week prior and kicked a bag filled with sand, breaking his ankle in the process. I felt no sympathy for him. I was angry about the whole affair leading up to my fight with Ives. I yelled down at him, "Yeah, I kicked your fighter's ass.

Who's next? I'll kick anybody's ass you put in front of me." He just looked up and smiled at me. At the end, instead of giving me a belt, some wannabe celebrity handed me a trophy. It was so small, you couldn't even see it when I held it in my gloved hand. I barked down to Danny, "I don't want no cheap trophy. Bring me the belt!"

I was still in the ring, full of adrenalin, when an old man came up to me and said, "Hey, how come you hate my son?"

I told him, "Who's your son?"

He responded, "The kid you just fought."

"Because, he has what I want!"

"What's that?"

I told him, "The 'W,' the win, the belt, the championship. He shouldn't have got in the ring with me in the first place."

They ended up carrying Mark out of the ring and straight to the hospital. He couldn't walk. I had hurt him with leg kicks to the body and thighs. I guess Danny realized that I was for real and wouldn't turn away from any fight. He began promoting me in other championship fights.

Years later, I was inducted into the IKBA Black Belt Hall of Fame as a fighter. Danny Rodarte, his son, Steve, and Master Richard Nuñez were inducted as promoters. Mark showed up at the event and trainer Frank Trejo too. I had no ill will against Mark and got to shake his hand as a fellow kickboxer. I found out Mark retired after our fight. They tried to talk him out of retirement, but for whatever reason he declined and never fought again.

I was nominated at different times as a fighter, trainer, and promoter for the Black Belt Hall of Fame, held in Las Vegas, Nevada. Besides my championships, I had been fortunate to have many of my students who became champions during the 1980s. But the induction fee was $2,000 for each nomination.

Years later, when I was working as a clerk for an attorney in Rancho Cucamonga, the attorney said he would have paid if he had known me when I was fighting. He quipped, "Everyone pays for their induction. Man, you and I could have made a lot of money back then." He thought it was important that I be honored and recognized for my work in martial arts. I humbly agreed, but I just didn't think it was right to pay for induction. I realize that the money was to help offset the cost for hotel, meals, entertainment, and plaques. Maybe I'm old fashioned or just cheap. But in my mind, I shouldn't have had to pay. Besides, I simply couldn't afford it at the time. I was proud to have at least been nominated.

THE CHAMPIONSHIP FIGHTS

Rodarte liked to use the Culver City Auditorium because it was centrally located for many martial arts schools in southern California. I fought for him a few more times. I went up in weight to 132 pounds and fought this guy from Tijuana by the name of Martin Márin. He was a boxer who seemed to be just learning to kickbox. He was trained by Angel Gutierrez, a well-known martial arts fighter in Mexico.

Angel and I were supposed to fight years before. But when he approached me with an offer to "buy" the belt, I told him, "Fuck you, I don't throw a fight for nobody." Angel fought Yohan Kim, and Kim knocked him out. I had wanted to fight Yohan too. Abe Belardo was his trainer. Abe was a fair and honest trainer. He told me, "You will never fight him, because you would knock him out." Abe meant it, I guess, because the fight never happened.

I fought Angel's fighter, Márin, and knocked him out in the first round. I dropped him with my hands. He got up, and I just missed him with kicks. I was trying to take his head off when I saw the towel being thrown in from his corner to stop the fight. He should've stayed in boxing.

I now had two titles, the California Lightweight and Junior Lightweight belts under the IKBA. Promoters now realized that I wouldn't back out of fights. I had the titles and was willing to put them up against anyone. Fighters not showing up or leaving tournaments before a big match occurred often. For example, I had a fighter from my school, he was one of my top prospects. He liked to call himself, "All World." But he would always have an excuse to drop out of fights. I called him, "All Mouth."

A lot of fighters are superstitious. They have habits that can't be changed, or it affects their confidence. Like professional baseball pitchers that jump over the chalk line for fear of bad luck if they touch it. I had to challenge my fighter. "Why are you dropping out of these fights right in the middle of competitions? I trained you, I know you can fight. I wouldn't let you compete if I didn't think you could win." My fighter eventually changed his attitude and attendance at tournaments and became one of my better fighters.

I knew Danny Rodarte was not the most honorable man in the world. Perhaps, none of us can really make that claim. I considered him to be the "Don King" of kickboxing. He was always hustling to make money and put together fights that he could control. I had to pay attention when he offered me bouts. I didn't care who I was fighting, but I also wanted a fair payday for it. I was grateful to him because he had opened the door to kickboxing for me.

Refugio and Jesús Flores had been a big help during my fight career. Refugio taught me better ways to train fighters and students. I didn't need to be overly disciplined and tough on my students like Master Sal had been with me. The Flores brothers remained under GM Ed Parker's Kenpo system until his death. At the time, they were seeking a partnership with a martial art association. I approached Myron Tuiolosega, who was now the head of the Tuiolosega International Lima Lama Organization Association (TILOA), to see if he would consider having the Flores Kenpo Karate school under our banner. Myron wanted the Flores Brothers to remove their patch and only use the LimaLama patch. I disagreed.

If we called ourselves an association, why would we require other schools to leave their original martial art style to join us? The Flores Brothers Kenpo Karate Studio could recognize both patches. GM Tino had done this many times with other schools. I couldn't convince the Tuiolosega brothers. They refused to accept the Flores brothers under the LimaLama banner unless they removed their Kenpo patches. Rightfully, Refugio and Jesús declined the TILOA offer and remained independent. They continued to train students at their school, honoring their Kenpo origins. In my opinion, LimaLama had lost a great opportunity to partner with exceptional martial artists like Refugio and Jesús. Likewise, TILOA was hampered in expanding in the United States by refusing to acknowledge other fighting style patches.

One day, I got a call from Refugio, asking me if I wanted to fight in his shows. I agreed, and my first fight was with a guy from Bakersfield named Smiley Ivan. He was trained by Abe Belardo. It was a full-contact fight. Smiley had previously fought George Agnat for an ESPN fight promoted by the Flores brothers in Oxnard. For this fight, Smiley and I were on the undercard that night. George Agnat vs. Troy Dorsey was the main event.

When my fight started, I threw a kick to Smiley's head that missed but followed it with a spinning back knuckle that went to his head. I opened a big gash above his eye, and the referee stopped the fight. Smiley's corner contended that I had hit him with a forearm instead of the back knuckle. But after some discussion, they judges decided it was a legal blow, so I ended up winning. Unbeknownst to me, Smiley had already signed a contract to fight the following month in Canada. I guess he and Abe had assumed that he would just walk over me to get to their next fight. That was their mistake.

Abe Belardo called me to see if I would be interested in fighting with the team in Canada. I told him, "So you thought Smiley was just going to walk over me?"

Abe quickly responded, "We studied you and thought we had your techniques figured out. We didn't expect the back knuckle. That was our mistake."

I agreed to fight but had to drop down to 130 pounds to fight. This fight would be for the North American Kickboxing Title. I had weighed 132 for the Márin fight, so losing a few pounds would be easy. I had been envious of Benny "The Jet" Urquidez fighting international fights, and now I was being given that same opportunity. I was going to fly to another country to fight! I was excited and trained so hard, I dropped my weight down to 126 pounds. I was too far underweight and didn't realize it. I had trained my ass off!

We arrived in Kanloop, Canada. The promoter was Mike Miles. We were supposed to be kickboxing, not full-contact. Ismael Robles was the trainer for the main event championship. Ismael had flown in from Texas, and I remembered him from my days there. I was grateful to share some memories with him before I got in the ring with his fighter.

Before the fight, I knew I was too light and wouldn't make the weight. I was two pounds under the minimum. If I didn't make the weight, I could still fight, but not for the title. So, I went to the dressing room and put a bunch of rolled up quarters in my jockstrap cup. I weighed in with all my sweats and t-shirts on to give me more weight. I came in at just over 131 pounds. Everyone on my team was asking me, "How did you make weight?" I told them, "I drank a lot of water and ate a lot of food." I lied, and they probably knew it. It didn't matter, because I made weight and could fight for the title.

I remember being so anxious to fight. When I got in the ring, my adrenaline felt like it was overflowing in my body. The referee motioned for me and the Canadian fighter, Billy Chin, to center ring and told us, "Okay, this is for the North American Lightweight WKA 135-pound belt, and it's a full-contact fight."

I backed up. "Wait a minute. This is supposed to be kickboxing. It's a title fight."

The referee said, "No, only world title fights are allowed leg kicks. This is the North American title."

I backed off, angrily. "No man, I trained too hard to come here and not be able to kick to the legs."

Well, if you go to the legs, then I'm going to disqualify you."

I went back to my corner. "Abe, there's no leg kicks, man. I trained for leg kicks, man."

Abe told me, "So, it's easier for you. Kick him to the legs anyways."

When the fight started, we started mixing it up. All of a sudden, *Whack!* I kicked Billy in the leg. He jumped back, yelling, and the referee warned me if I kicked to the leg again, he would take a point from me. We started fighting again and I was trying to catch him with a spinning back knuckle. Billy was reading my movements and countering me. I tried to mix the back knuckle with some other moves and was able to finally catch him with some kicks. Billy put his leg out and I was tempted to hit it but instead pulled it, and immediately, *Pop*—he hit me with a hook and dropped me.

I was on the canvas, looking up, thinking, *What the fuck am I doing here? I should have just kicked him.* I got up and tried to go after him, but the referee stopped me and made me take a standing "eight count." Billy and I went back at it again and fought the full five rounds. I thought I had lost the fight because of the knockdown. But I had been so aggressive and accumulated so many points that I won the match and the title.

We went to a local pub after the fight and Billy came up to the table with a pitcher of beer. He told me, "Hey, I'd like to share this pitcher of beer with you. I've never got my ass beat so bad or had such a hard fight. We put on a hell of a fight."

I said, "Cool." The beer was too strong for me, so I just sipped one glass all night. If I had drunk more, I wouldn't have been able to get out of bed in the morning. I asked him how he was able to defend my spinning back knuckle. Billy told me that I always tipped my shoulder before I made my spin move. He just timed my moves to counter. He was a good fighter, and I had learned a lot from the fight.

I was in Santa Barbara for the Professional Kickboxing Association (PKA) 132-Pound Junior Lightweight division. It was 1982. The fighter, Anthony Childress, was supposedly the Las Vegas Champion and supposed to fight one of my students. I think he had gotten inside my student's head. It was a common thing among fighters at tournaments to psych-out opponents or intimidate them before a match. It happened to my student, who asked, "Why don't you fight Childress because he is a champion, like you, and I can fight your opponent instead?"

I figured, why not fight for a championship instead. I told him, "Sure, let's go ask the tournament sponsors to change the card." I told the promoter that I would put up my belt against his fighter. They agreed. We went toe to toe the first round. In the second round, I knocked him out with a kick to the head. It got a lot of media attention. They had to carry him out on a stretcher to the hospital. The newspapers called it the "Big scare at karate tournament." I fought Childress again in Oxnard a few months later.

BECOMING A CHAMPION

Childress had told his promoters that the knockout he suffered in Santa Barbara was a fluke and that I had been lucky to get the win. His trainer had called me and asked if I would be interested in a rematch for the title. I readily agreed. However, at the time, I had just fought for the vacant IKBA Featherweight title in Culver City. I knocked out my opponent in the first round. Since that fight had quickly ended, the promoters, Refugio and Jesús Flores, from the Flores Brothers Kenpo Karate Studio, agreed to allow me to fight again for the World Kickboxing Association (WKA) title against Childress. Jesús was the promoter, and Refugio was my trainer.

There had been a time prior to this fight when I wanted to fight Refugio for his World title belt in full-contact karate. I had a belt in another organization, and I wanted to take his belt. The fight never happened. Years later I mentioned it to Refugio, and he responded, "That would have been a great fight." I had the highest respect for Refugio. He was a great fighter, a humble and honest man.

The fight with the Flores Brothers fighter, Childress, would take place in Oxnard only one week after my knockout fight in Culver City. Childress and I were on the undercard for our rematch. The main event was George Agnat vs Juan "The Ghost Warrior" Torres. They were fighting for the WKA, 135-Pound Welterweight Championship. Juan Torres beat George that night.

Before the Oxnard fight, I approached Childress and told him, "This time, there is no fluke. I'm not going to knock you out, I'm going to hurt you. You don't have to worry about my right leg; it's the left leg you have to worry about. I won't knock you out, but I'm going to hurt you." During our bout. I knew I had gotten inside his head. He was already beaten and fought like it too. A couple of times, I grabbed him by the neck and acted like I was gonna knee him to the body. But I just threw him on the rope and hit him with combinations. I beat him badly each round because I stayed aggressive and wouldn't let him rest. He failed to make the mandatory eight kicks each round. The judge stopped the fight and disqualified him. I defended my PKA Junior Lightweight title and with this win had added the WKA Junior Lightweight title too.

THE JET CENTER

Around 1983–84, I met this guy named Sonny Hughes. Sonny was a black belt in jiu-jitsu and judo. He had watched some of my fights and wanted to meet me. Sonny started coming to my El Monte Self Defense School and watched my students train. Pretty soon he started helping me out, training students. He was a character. He didn't like to pay to go to fights, but he always found a way into the fighter's room. He always named-dropped celebrities and martial artists that he said he knew. I didn't believe him until one day he introduced me to David Lee Roth, a musician/singer who played with the Van Halen rock band. Sonny also said he trained with Benny "The Jet" Urquidez. That sparked my interest. Benny was already a well-known fighter in karate and kickboxing.

At the time, Robert Alcazar, my boxing trainer, was having problems at home. His time was split between training Oscar de la Hoya and having quality time with his family. So, to stay sharp and keep fighting in tournaments, I got help from a guy named Ronald Tucker. He was a big bald-headed weightlifting dude. He fought twice as a professional, winning both by knockout, but he was well known as a boxing trainer in Baldwin Park. Sonny also would help me in my corner for some boxing fights. Not long thereafter, Sonny introduced me to the Urquidez family. He took me to Benny's studio, a second-floor gym in a building in Van Nuys, before the Jet Center was built.

The Urquidez family really made an impact with me in different ways. I was probably closer to Ruben and Blinky, who seemed to be handling most of the business and promotion ends of the Urquidez Gym. Ruben was a great fight promoter and wanted me to be part of the Urquidez fight team. We co-promoted a lot of fights. They took some "smoker" tournaments that were too large for my gym. And I would assist them with a large tournament called "Night of the Heavyweights." It went smooth, with about 15 fights. Another one was called the "Beauty and the Beasts." Ruben and I became close friends. Eventually, the Urquidez family invited my El Monte school to be part of the Jet Center. My gym would have been called the Jet Center #2. But I couldn't afford the franchise costs.

Blinky was married to Lilly Urquidez. Blinky was a competitive martial artist in karate and kickboxing who had fought in the super middleweight championship fights against the best. I remember, one time he sparred with me to help me prepare for a tournament. He was trying to polish my left hooks when he hit me and cracked one of my ribs in the process. When we got together, we'd always be talking strategy for fights. Benny's sister Lilly was also an influence in my kickboxing training. She was a black belt in Kenpo, Shotokan, and judo who had many championship fights under her belt. She helped me polish my footwork as a kickboxer. The Urquidez family was eventually able to build a state-of-the-art facility in San Fernando called the Jet Center.

Benny was always busy. He'd fly around the world to compete against the best fighters, advise Hollywood actors for fight movies, or make special appearances at promotional events. He brought kickboxing to the forefront of martial arts. I was fortunate to see him at the Jet Center on occasion when I'd be training. The Jet Center was visited by the elite champions of karate and kickboxing. You had to be somebody in the martial arts community to be able to train there. I already had a few belts under me and was starting to be noticed by other promoters. My training in kickboxing needed to be enhanced. Fortunately, I learned a better way to prepare for fights with Benny as a mentor.

L-R: Benny "The Jet" Urquidez, Jessie 'Surgeon' Serna, and Lorenzo "Coach" Rodriguez.

I was lucky to spar with him a few times over the period I trained at the Jet Center. But when we sparred, we'd really go at it, and I always walked away having learned something from Benny. I appreciated the beating he gave me. I recall training one day at the Jet Center facility. I was hitting the bag hard with kicks and punches. Benny came up to me and said, "What are you doing?"

I stopped punching, looked at him and responded, "I'm training."

"Why?"

"Because I have a fight coming up."

"Yeah, but why are you training so hard?"

I was ready for this question, I had years of sparring and fighting experience that taught me how to train. "Because how you train, is how you fight."

He shook his head from side to side, and said, "Train smart, fight smart." He then proceeded to show me how to cut the kicks and pull the punches. "This is how you work your way inside. Don't wear yourself out before your fight. Be at your best condition when the fight starts."

I had always trained hard with the intent to go full blast in competition. If I noticed a weakness in a fighter's technique during the fight, then I would capitalize on the vulnerability. Benny had fought in international tournaments against the very best. He would tell me in detail about a fight he had in Germany or one in Japan and how he changed his stance or technique to wear down his opponent. He showed me that training smarter would give me an advantage in the ring.

He made sense. But it made more sense when I got in the ring with him. He proved it to me.

One time, I was sparring with Benny. He hit me with a solid uppercut. It was so clean, I said, "Do it again." If he had wanted to knock my ass out, he could have, but he didn't.

He said, "Look, I can hit you clean, but I don't have to hurt you. You can spar without hurting your sparring partner."

I realized that I could still feel a little of the pain from getting hit, but not enough to hurt me. He taught me how to train better. To conserve my power for tournaments without sacrificing my timing and rhythm. At the time, my fight mentality was simple: I'm going to work on my combinations, work the circuit and then go out and bang in the ring. As a result, I was winning. I didn't know there was more to the fight game. I believed you train as hard as you fight. And I had always trained hard. That was my Limalama experience—you got to feel it to learn it.

It was still true, only now Benny was explaining that you didn't have to feel *all of the pain*. Because, if you did, what would you have left? You'd only get beat up from training before you ever entered a ring. Benny was an absolute scholar of fight tactics and strategy. His knowledge of martial arts and application in tournaments was unrivaled.

MY LAST CHAMPIONSHIP FIGHT

In 1985, another tournament was held in Northridge. The Jet Center promoted the fight. This would be my sixth fight promoted under the Jet Center and, unbeknownst to me, my last. I had been going to the Jet Center once or twice a week to train. Robert Alcazar was still my coach. We trained really hard. My opponent was Lawrence Miera, from New Mexico, in the super featherweight division. Benny was fighting a guy named Tom LaRoche from Canada. Years later, LaRoche would take on Ismael Robles for the World Kickboxing Championship. He went on to make three title defenses, and then retired the champion. My opponent, Miera, was trained by Al Chavez. He always had his fighters well prepared for fights. I knew I was going to be in a great fight and was excited to get in the ring.

I was stretching in the back room with another fighter, John "The Train" Hickelman. John asked me if I would help him warm up. John weighed 185 pounds, and I was at 126 pounds. This was common among fighters, to get stretched and blood flowing just before entering the ring. But if my trainer, Robert Alcazar, had seen us warming up, he would have chewed my ass out. Robert was really protective of me.

John was the 18-year trainer and sparring partner for MMA champion Chuck Ladell. At one time, John Hickelman and Chuck Ladell had fought each other in karate tournaments.

John was a recognized black belt trained in Kajukenbo and a former boxer in the Army who developed a unique MMA training regime called "The Pit." The Pit has trained many top-ranked fighters, like Peter "Sugarfoot" Cunningham, Joe Lewis, Cecil Peoples, Matt Lindland, Dave Camarillo, Cesar Gracie, Paul Buentello, Josh Thomson, and most of the guys I knew from the American Kickboxing Academy.

Peter 'Sugarfoot' Cunningham (L) and Lorenzo "Coach" Rodriguez (R).

Some years later, I trained in John's Pit Academy in Arroyo Grande, California, and even joined the *Pit Pro-Am Kickboxing Team* in Temecula, California, for a short period. It was a good training program. Only the best MMA fighters could attend. John was training gladiators. I got to work with Chuck Ladell on the focus gloves one time. I also trained in jiu-jitsu for ground-and-pound techniques. I never liked it—having a guy's sweaty body on top of me—but I did it. The academy gave me a blue belt from the "Pit," which didn't mean anything to me. A belt for *training* is not the same as a belt earned in a deadly martial art.

I had finished my hand-boxing warmups and was about to start warming my legs up. John and I squared off. We started sparring lightly, and I threw a left leg kick to the head. I pulled the kick on purpose because we were only warming up. I shouldn't have; he blocked it with a right hand and threw a kick to my supporting leg. *Pow!* My knee popped out, and I fell back to the floor. I had torn my meniscus tendon. I quickly pushed it back in and wrapped it. Hickelman apologized as I finished taping it up. But in that instance, all my energy seemed to have been sucked out of me. I had to fight off the feeling, but I couldn't seem to totally shake it loose.

I didn't tell anybody about it, because I had trained so fucking hard for this fight and wanted to fight. Robert Alcazar came into the room and saw my knee wrapped up and asked why I had wrapped my knee. I told him, "Don't worry about it. It's my bad knee. It gave me a little tingle, so I wrapped it up." But I knew better. My body felt drained of energy. I was going to go out to the ring and battle some guy, and I was already hurt. If it had been any of my fighters, I wouldn't have let them fight. But since it was me, nobody was going to tell me not to fight.

So I went out there and fought. Miera was a good fighter, and his trainer, Al Chavez, was an excellent trainer. At the championship level, everyone in the fight game knows each other. It is small community of fighters, trainers, and promoters. You knew who the best trainers were and who wasn't. You knew who was bringing "tomato cans" (nobodies) to a fight. Miera was somebody. And I knew it.

BECOMING A CHAMPION

Smiley, Benny's brother, was the referee for the fight. I already had a noticeable limp during the fight. Miera dropped me with a punch in the second round. I got up and Smiley gave me an eight-count, keeping me from going after Miera. From this point on, I knew I could only move forward. I had no balance in my leg for side-to-side movement. Miera clipped me with a left hook. Miera had an excellent left hook and was a polished boxer. I was in for a tough fight.

Miera kicked me in the groin three different times. I got an eight-count each time. Smiley warned him about the kicks, but it didn't matter. I was more concerned about my bad knee than my balls. Sometime later, after my fight with Miera, referees in tournaments started giving fighters more time to recover after groin shots.

In the third round, and as I stepped back, I fell down. My knee just gave out. I had to push my knee back in and get back up. But when I got back up, my body had nothing left. It was that feeling you get when you leave the sauna room. Your body is totally drained. I ignored my body and mixed it up again with Miera. I was throwing strikes, but I had no power behind my punches. My kicks were useless; psychologically, my body fought to protect my injured knee. My heart said "fight," but my mind knew better.

In the fourth round, Smiley stopped the fight. I pushed Smiley out of the way to get after Miera. I was angry. I told Smiley, "Don't stop the fight, take a point. Let me go after him. I can fight." Smiley refused and waved me off to the judges. He wouldn't let the fight continue.

Afterwards, I watched the fight on tape, and realized that Smiley had given me a lot of time. He was right to have stopped the fight. Even if I had wanted to hurt Miera, my leg was so trashed, it wasn't going to make a difference in the outcome. I approached Smiley and apologized for pushing him. I told him, "You did the right thing in stopping the fight. I shouldn't have pushed you. I was wrong." He understood my mindset. I was a fighter and never wanted to accept defeat. But Miera had beaten me. My knee was no excuse for the loss. I went in that fight to kick Miera's ass and only ended up getting my own ass beat. It was a good fight.

Once my knee started getting better. I wanted a rematch with Miera. I trained and trained, trying to set up the rematch. It was taking too long. Al Chavez later confided to me that he had to go and convince Miera to fight again. Al said that Miera had taken a beating from me. But I knew I had taken one from him too. The fight never happened. It would have been a great fight.

I continued to train hard, but I couldn't get any more fights on my terms. A lot of promoters who offered me fights wanted to pay their fighters more money than me. The fighters were undefeated and unranked. I understood the game. They were protecting their fighters from unnecessary losses. Promoters told me, more than a few times, "Look Lorenzo, I know you can beat my fighter. I have to protect my interests and get paid. If my guy loses, it will be harder for him to get good fights." I felt I was a recognized champion and deserved to be paid the same or more than other fighters. In my heart, I felt I was worthy of a champion's respect and refused to be treated as anything less.

I finally decided to hang up the gloves after a last-minute call, around 1991, offering me to be a "fill-in" for a championship fight in Las Vegas, Nevada. I was 36 years old and didn't have the same passion for tournament fights anymore. I turned down the fight. It wasn't an easy decision. Every fighter wants to go out on top. Some fighters never know when to hang up the gloves.

But I knew it was time. I had spent over 10 years fighting in kickboxing competitions. I had been a champion in three separate weight divisions. I was still a martial artist with ranking in LimaLama. I had nothing more to prove in the streets, gym, or tournaments. It was time to teach the next generation of warriors. I decided to focus on preparing my students to be champions themselves and representing my school at the highest level in the martial arts community.

TRAINING UNDER GRANDMASTER TINO

GM Tino disappeared for a number of years. It was the primary reason I couldn't reach out to him to confirm my status as a LimaLama black belt. No one from the LimaLama community knew or was aware of his location. He was already an urban legend among his martial arts peers, and there were plenty of tales explaining his absence from the martial arts community. Stories of a Yakuza death sentence, Russian or Armenian crime gangs chasing him, or a mafia debt that hadn't been paid. Some said he had moved to Europe or South America. Others thought he might be in jail or dead. Whatever the reason, it didn't matter. He was gone from us for a period of about seven years.

When word came that the Father of Kenpo Karate in the United States, Ed Parker, had passed away, GM Tino returned from the shadows to attend his close friend's funeral. My friend Hector Ventoura reached out to me to attend the funeral. On behalf of the TILOA, I bought a large funeral wreath for the burial service. Not long after the funeral, GM Tino gathered his black belts together for a meeting in Santa Cruz, California. No mention was made about his long absence, and we were all curious about why we had been summoned. The first thing GM Tino did was tell all of us to remove our gi tops. He then passed out shirts that introduced a new patch and name, *Kenpo Si Lama*.

Some of the original students questioned why the change was needed. Was it a nod to Ed Parker's legacy? GM Tino allowed the masters in attendance to keep their school patches, but they were asked to add the new patch design to their gi. We may never know the reason for the change in our name, but the basic principles of LimaLama, distinct from Kenpo Karate, had remained intact. The new techniques seemed to be variations of all our previous LimaLama forms. Many of the masters in attendance were not happy with having to start over in a "new" art. Many quietly asked each other, "Why are we doing this?"

In my mind, LimaLama wasn't changing except for the name. I suspected GM Tino may have had some legal dispute over copyright ownership of the name, which made him change it to protect himself. I really don't know or care. I was simply happy that our grandmaster had returned to us.

Prior to finally seeing GM Tino at Ed Parker's funeral. I had made friends with one of GM Tino's black belt students. He was a Samoan named Zachery. He worked as a security guard at her high school. Everyone called him "Laca." One of my students who attended the high school found out that Zachary was a black belt under GM Tino Tuiolosega. She shared with Laca that she was a student in LimaLama.

All this time, I had been trying to get hold of GM Tino and had hit nothing but dead ends. Master Sal had told me that GM Tino was aware of my school's existence and that I had been blackballed for breaking away from LimaLama. He made it clear that GM Tino wanted nothing to do with me. I refused to believe Master Sal's version of anything having to do with my school or GM Tino. I had to know for myself what GM Tino thought about me and my school. I needed to hear from him the truth about my status. Now that GM Tino had returned, it was time for me to meet with him directly.

I asked my student if she would introduce me to Zachery. I eventually met him, and we became friends. He would train with me at my school. He was as tall as GM Tino but not as big or as fast. Zachary was strong and definitely knew his shit. He was a great guy who had been trained in LimaLama only. Like me, he had no other martial arts training before learning LimaLama. He showed me a few of the different techniques GM Tino had taught him, and we began to attend tournaments together. He would introduce me to other black belts in LimaLama, like Greg Spence. Eventually, "Zach," as I called him, set up a meeting with GM Tino at his home.

We sat at GM Tino's kitchen table. I explained to GM Tino all that had occurred between Master Sal and me. I told him all I ever taught to my students was LimaLama, nothing more. I wanted to know if I was really teaching LimaLama. The only way I would know for sure is if I was studying under him. I said, "You are the founder of LimaLama, and I don't want to come here and train with you and have the fear others have of you. I respect you and I want to learn correctly and go under you."

GM Tino responded, "Well, I've had other black belts come to me from other organizations and even from Sal's schools. Then they go back and never stay with me. How do I know you aren't going to do that?"

"I've been with Sal since I started. And I didn't leave because I wanted too. He kicked me out. If I say I will be loyal to you, then I will be loyal to you, no matter what. But I don't want to be ruled by fear, I want to be ruled by knowledge." I said that to him, remembering that Masters Sal and Richard would routinely take pain medications before training with GM Tino. They were afraid of him, knowing he demanded they fight him when training. He was a powerful man. It didn't take much for him to injure someone.

GM Tino looked at me and said, "Sal is one of my students, but he's doing his own thing."

I'm in the middle, Tino. I am going to keep teaching, but wouldn't you prefer that when I say, 'I'm teaching LimaLama,'

I say that it is your system? You are the founder of LimaLama. If you teach me, I'm not going to say, like others have said, 'I want to be like Bruce Lee.' Because then I would become a clone. Tino, if you train me, I don't want to be like you. I want to be better than you." I could see GM Tino didn't like what I just said.

GM Tino stared directly at me before he spoke. "Are you finished?"

"Yes."

He waved his finger at me, saying, "You will never, ever talk to me like this again. This is the first and last time I will hear about all this. I will take you under my wing. You will come here every Saturday and train with me. And I will charge you. But, if you go back to Sal or go away from me, you're gonna see the bad side of me."

I responded, "There have been black belts and others who wanted me to join their organizations. But I have remained loyal to LimaLama. It is all I know. I have represented LimaLama in Korea and in Texas. It's all I know. I have proudly represented LimaLama all this time and will continue to represent LimaLama. I want to teach what you teach."

GM Tino had accepted me as his student. He taught LimaLama but had no formal curriculum, no set forms or progressions like you see at many martial arts studios. GM Tino only taught techniques he felt I should work on and master for that particular training class. Once he determined that I had mastered the form or techniques, only then did he introduce another one. He was so strong, he only used his fingers when he'd strike. If he used his hands, he could hurt me. Sometimes he did use hands just to keep me alert. It didn't matter; I soaked it all in like a sponge.

GM Tino and Lorenzo Rodriguez, practicing LimaLama forms, circa 1993.

Like the Chinese Ba Gua Sifu I studied under while stationed in Korea, GM Tino never sparred. I would get in front of him, and he would show me a technique. He expected me to attack him with all my force giving 100 percent effort. If I didn't, he would hurt me for not giving my all. If I used all my effort to punch or kick him, he still hurt me, but not as much. He would continually remind me, "You better try to hit me." Only after I had felt the power of his strikes would he then walk me through the form or technique.

There were always multiple applications for the same hand or body movements. His ferocious teaching method demonstrated two things: first, how effective the technique was; and secondly, how easily you could vary the same hand, wrist, arm, or leg application to injure your attacker. I realized what I had always suspected: LimaLama wasn't meant to be an internal martial art. The fighting art GM Tino had created had no medicinal or spiritual benefits. It was simply a deadly art. And I wanted to master it.

LimaLama has no blocks; they are all strikes. Its defense is its offense. When your enemy attempts to attack you, you hit him with combinations. It could begin as a strike to the arm or leg to stop the initial attack coming at you. But you continue striking the head or body, moving straight forward or angling forward, left or right at your adversary, depending on their actions. You are always moving forward against your opponent. LimaLama fighting principles demand that you finish the battle as quickly as it started.

GGM Tino would demonstrate multiple applications, from the same technique to different parts of the body, depending on the reaction or movement of the attacker. LimaLama strikes weren't intended to just cause pain to thwart an enemy. They were meant to cause injury to stop the attack or end the immediate danger. Simply put, when an arm, leg, nose, jaw, etc. is broken, it can no longer be used against you.

As I progressed under him, he promoted me in degrees. It was the hardest training I'd been under but the most rewarding because I was learning directly from the founder of LimaLama. Most days, I'd train for six to eight hours with GGM Tino and then break for lunch or dinner before assisting him in training other black belt students. Many nights I'd sleep at his house to begin again the next morning.

L-R: Myrion Tuiolosega, GM Tino Tuiolosega, Master Alan Lopez, Master Greg Spence, and me, Lorenzo "Coach" Rodriguez, circa 1998.

There were days he'd have me stand in the horse position for hours in his garage, just as the Chinese Sifu of Ba Gua had done in Korea. This basic position is meant to establish balance and strengthen the legs. It is also a test to see if you will follow the instructions of the master. GM Tino trained some very accomplished and well-known martial artists, and he treated them the same way. It didn't matter who you were, he was always going to test you to see if you really were committed to learning LimaLama.

Students who gave up or refused to continue in the horse stance were not considered to be committed to the art and eventually left. I never refused any instruction from masters when I trained. Sometimes, I suspected GM Tino had forgotten about me, but I wasn't about to break the horse pose only to find out that it was another test of my endurance and patience. I remained in the pose until he'd return to begin the technique instructions for that day. This routine happened nearly every weekend. I'd spend the next day resting from the strikes I had sustained all over my body. GM Tino always found a way to exhaust my energy. I loved every brutal minute of it. I trained with GM Tino for five straight years. I was honored to have earned multiple levels ending with the 8th degree under his tutelage. Fighters don't always age well and I sadly lost my 'Papa' Tino to the heavens in 2011.

I was proud to represent LimaLama and GM Tino then and more so today, as I continue to honor our art and grandmaster as a trainer and teacher. The belief that LimaLama can continue to improve and adapt into a better fighting system was not lost on our grandmaster, and that notion has remained with me to this day.

5

THE NEXT GENERATION

SMOKERS AND THE MIGHTY MITES

WHEN I HAD MY own school in El Monte, I had been actively training and competing in kickboxing tournaments, trying to make a name for myself as a professional. I had two passions. First, to get bigger fights to reach national and international recognition. Second, for my students to be dominant in kickboxing tournaments. I wanted my students to fight and not worry about the judges' scoring. They were expected to put "hands" on their opponent so that they would be remembered long after the fight was over.

In my opinion, kickboxing offered the best avenue to showcase the skills of LimaLama and the overall fighting ability of my students. It allowed kicks to nearly the entire body and full contact on strikes. I and my students always gave the crowds an entertaining fight. We were aggressive and didn't focus on scoring points. We wanted to bang with the opponent and beat them up. The crowds knew it and always watched to see if we'd get a knockout or disqualified for illegal blows.

When I was approached at local tournaments, the LimaLama patch was easily recognized and respected. Former masters Richard Nuñez and Sal Esquivel had accomplished GM Tino's vision to raise LimaLama's prestige in the martial arts community. With each generation, LimaLama grew in recognition as a ferocious fighting art. When asked, I spoke proudly about the art, my students, and the El Monte Self Defense School for martial arts. I taught many students over a period of 25 years in El Monte.

Promotional photo of Lorenzo "Coach" Rodriguez, circa 1982.

THE NEXT GENERATION

When I moved from one location to another in El Monte, my students came with me. When I didn't have a school and only taught from my garage, many fighters still came to train in LimaLama or kickboxing. One of my students told me that people would say, "If you want to learn Muay Thai, go to Moreno Valley and this little Mexican guy will teach you to fight. My backyard had two rings, and my garage had all the bags and mats to properly train. The students recognized the intensity of my conditioning regime and the quality of the students I prepared for fights.

At one time, I held a number of PKA and WKA titles in featherweight and lightweight kickboxing championships. But I was much prouder that some of my students had earned the heavyweight, cruiserweight, and middleweight titles too. My school had established a reputation for training good fighters in LimaLama and kickboxing.

Every Friday, we had open sparring. Students would pay $5 to $10, and they could spar with other students. When everyone got tired or quit, I'd end the session. It got to be really popular, and other school began to attend the sparring sessions. By 1986–87, the sparring sessions became "smokers." I invited other schools to bring their students to the smokers. Eventually, all the schools began promoting their own smokers, and competition between the schools became the norm.

The term *smokers* started in the 1920s and '30s. Bars, barns, and old vacant buildings were used to stage boxing matches. Everyone in attendance would be drinking and smoking—especially rich guys smoking long cigars and betting on young fighters. All the smoke in the air is what gave those fights the name, *smokers*. During the Depression, guys fought to make a little money to feed themselves and their families. If they won, they got paid a little more. There was a purpose for wanting to win. These guys were fighting to live, to feed their families.

The smoker sparring sessions I started were unsanctioned fights because the state commission wasn't regulating them. I wanted to avoid the state commission fee and oversite rules. The smokers were conducted like the underground fights from the Depression era, and in the dive bars of Korea, when I had fought for the colonel.

Now I was the one promoting underground fights in California. The difference between the Depression smokers and mine was twofold. First, there was no smoking allowed; and second, no one was fighting for their lives. My students were fighting for self-pride and the honor of representing our school. They loved the full-contact combat against other belts their own age and weight. We had some spirited fights that began to draw good crowds.

Not long after the smokers got popular, some of my students complained, "Why don't we get something for our fights?" It made sense to give them something to take home besides bumps and bruises.

I told them, "I will make trophies for the competition. We will make it like a karate tournament, and I will charge you to compete."

I paid to have the Amateur Athletic Union (AAU), Chinese Boxing Club, as our sanctioning body. They provided insurance coverage for our fights. It was a legal way for my students to get experience in full-contact fighting and get a trophy for their efforts. The state commission couldn't fine or impose their rules or referees on our competitions. Likewise, no doctors or ambulance would be required under the AAU umbrella. It saved us a lot of money, and I used the money I made from the smokers to pay the rent for my school.

The politics surrounding the fight game never made much sense to me. In boxing, kids 10 years old and up were allowed to compete in tournaments. But in martial arts you had to be

THE NEXT GENERATION

16 to compete. I didn't think it was fair. The state commission set an arbitrary age limit without any rationale to support why that age was appropriate. I wanted to start something for our younger students 15 and younger. So, I created the Mighty Mites program for kickboxing around 1987. The kids in Mighty Mites were required to wear body protection, shin guards, gloves, and headgear. They fought five one-minute rounds with a one-minute rest.

The smokers' competition became the "Fair Tournament." We gave every participant a trophy for competing. It didn't matter if you won or lost. It gave the kids a sense of pride for having participated in a tournament. It also gave them experience in fighting in front of a crowd. It became really popular, and other schools started having them too. I tried to organize it with the other schools so that we could all maximize attendance by not staging Fair Tournaments at the same time. It seemed no one was interested because all the schools wanted to make a fast buck, so it never became a reality.

The El Monte Self Defense School for martial arts had established a reputation of tough and talented fighters at competitions. Soon, all my success became a curse to me to get quality fights. A lot of promoters wouldn't let me face their fighters at tournaments because they wanted to protect their records, especially if they were undefeated. The same thing happened with my students. It was getting harder and harder to find fights for them too. When a promoter did call me, I'd make them take at least two of my fighters for the undercard. Finally, I realized it would be easier if I promoted my own tournaments. I could make a little money and keep my fighters busy.

As my Fair Tournaments grew, I asked Ruben Urquidez if I could hold some at the Jet Center because the crowd was getting too big for my school to accommodate. Eventually, Ruben and I conducted some major tournaments at the Jet Center.

One was called *Beauty and the Beasts*. We had a few female kickboxers and some heavyweight bouts. It turned out to be one of the best tournaments in southern California.

I started promoting fighters professionally around the early 1990s. Ruben had introduced me to Howard Hansen, President of the World Kickboxing Association (WKA). Hansen appointed me as a WKA representative. I was fortunate to take teams to different parts of the United States, including Canada and Mexico. I took about five teams to Mexico over a four-year period. Some promoters in Mexico would try to send professional fighters to the amateur tournaments I had organized. I would remind them that I had sent them fighters equal in skill and experience. If they tried to put an A-fighter, their best fighter, against my B- or C-fighter, I told them, "Don't try to set up my fighters for a loss. If you do that, I'll fuck you up." I was a promoter, and my fighters came first. They knew I meant business if they tried to advance their fighters at my students expense.

I brought fighters to Mexico to give them experience and showcase kickboxing, I didn't bring them to tournaments to get their ass kicked. If the promoter tried to take advantage by mismatching the fighters, then we were going to have some fun kicking their ass outside the ring. Most promoters were previously fighters and they knew about my reputation for meaning exactly what I said. Thankfully, it never happened. But a few tried to set up easy fights before I stepped in to stop it.

MIGUEL REYES

Miguel Reyes, the Mexican kickboxing champion, had a large sparring gym in Tijuana. He was a really good fighter. He was an accountant by trade and later became a trainer. Miguel was a black belt in LimaLama who had trained directly under GM Rigoberto Lopez. Miguel and I had become good friends over the years. One time I took some fighters to Tijuana to purchase fight gear. One of the fighters was a small guy, and the other fighter was a heavyweight. The heavyweight was a big dude about six feet five and weighing over 275 pounds. I called Miguel to join us for lunch at Puerto Nuevo in Baja California. But he told us that Jackie Nava owned a restaurant in Rosarito that sold good lobster too. Jackie Nava was a World Boxing Council champion. He was right, they cooked the lobster six different ways. What I didn't know was that the little fighter didn't eat seafood. Luckily, the restaurant found him a steak. We all had a delicious time.

Miguel told us that one of the guys from Tijuana, called Eric "Terrible" Morales was fighting in Las Vegas. Eric was a lightweight boxer, and the fight would be televised. Miguel invited us to go watch the fight and party at his place, and we were welcome to spend the night if it got late. But the heavyweight was too scared to go. We had driven across the border in his car. He told me he hadn't told his wife that he would be staying overnight. But he admitted that he was afraid of Tijuana, after all the stories he heard about what they do to American tourists.

The guy was huge. His arm was the size of both my legs. If you remember the actor Michael Clarke Duncan, from the movie *The Green Mile*, that is how big he was. I told him, "You scared? What are you afraid of? You're bigger than all of us. Look, it's rare when someone invites you into their home like this without advance notice. It's an honor to be invited to someone's house. You have nothing to be afraid of."

Miguel tried to convince him too. "We are gonna have carne asada, frijoles, arroz, and drinks. Vamanos, amigo." (Let's go, friend.) "We have plenty of room for everyone." But it didn't matter. The big guy was too scared.

The heavyweight pulled me aside, "Coach, "Please don't leave me alone, okay? Here, in this country, I'm lost, man. I don't speak the language."

I looked up at him. "Shit, you think anybody is going to mess with you. You're supposed to be protecting me."

"Yeah, but I heard about the cops and how they treat you."

"Listen, LimaLama masters in Tijuana train the cops over here. Besides, the police already gave us a 'key to the city' the last time we came. It's good for a year. We got it made over here. The only thing you can't do here is kill someone or sell drugs."

Unfortunately, it didn't matter what we said. He was our driver, and he refused to stay overnight. We ended up coming back home to the United States. I was disappointed to have missed a home-cooked Mexican meal.

JUNKYARD BRAWL

I was contacted by a Miami promoter, as the WKA representative, and asked if I could get a Mexican team to compete in the Junkyard Brawl amateur tournament in Miami, Florida. The promotion was Mexico vs. the United States. The promoter had secured a lot of Mexican restaurants and radio sponsors for the amateur tournament. The tournament was a WKA-sanctioned fight. Under WKA rules, leg kicks are allowed. As always, I prepared my fighters to attack and trained them in kicking the legs. The fight winners would be taken to Europe to compete for world title belts. This was going to be a great opportunity for me as a promoter.

I took Miguel, Johnny 'Z' Zea and David "Wild Thing" Morrow as my Mexican team to Florida. I worked with all of them for the tournament. They were all black belts. Miguel and I were the only true Mexicans on our team. Johnny was an independent fighter in Kempo. Guatemalans called their martial art *Guatekempo*. David was a black belt in taekwondo. David was a United States citizen but had Native American features. He spoke no Spanish. Between us, Miguel, Johnny, and I could speak Spanish. As long as no one asked where we were from, I figured we could get away with it. I was wrong.

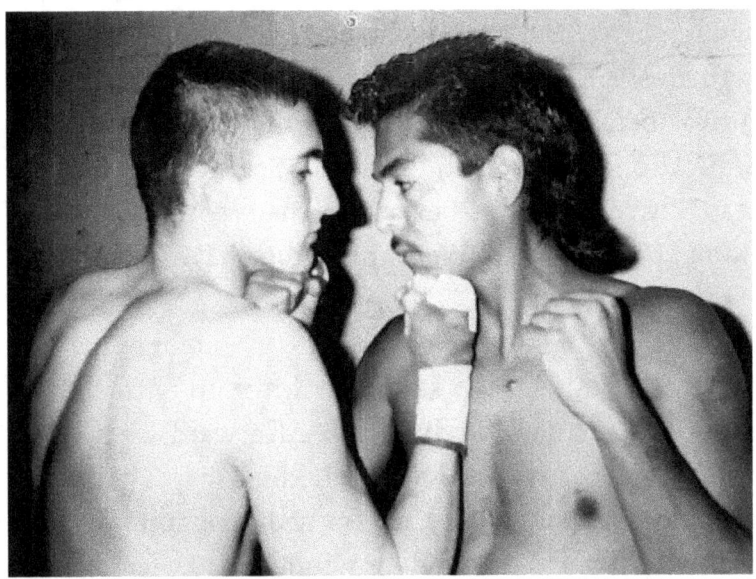

Craig 'The Bullet' Buchanan (L) and David "Wild Thing" Morrow (R).

When we arrived, the promoter wasn't going to feed us. It had always been my experience that the tournament promoter took care of room and board for fighters. But not in this tournament. I told the promoter, "No, this is bullshit. It's your job to take care of the fighters coming from out of town. I'll remember this when you want to come to California." Fortunately, many of the sponsors were local Mexican restaurants, and they fed all of us. Otherwise, I would have had to pick up the bill. The promoter took us to radio stations to promote the fight. We are supposed to invite the public on the airways to come join the tournament. Johnny Zea didn't want to talk because he had a speech impediment, a cleft lip that made it difficult to understand him. David Morrow didn't speak a word of Spanish, and I spoke broken Spanish, having lived most of my life in the United States. Miguel was the only true Spanish-speaking fighter.

Miguel tried to respond to the questions, but the radio personalities tried to get all of us to speak. Johnny was too embarrassed to speak, and I think they recognized his difficulty. So, they turned to David for answers. I tried to whisper to David what was being said and answer on his behalf. But the sponsors questioned why he didn't speak Spanish. David believed he was Native American, but he was just another Chicano who couldn't speak Spanish. We were glad to have gotten through the radio interviews.

Finally, they took us to a very large gym where the tournament would be held. We start matching up with the Miami fighters and made introductions. Afterwards, I wanted to loosen up my team. We pulled out the Muay Thai pads and started kicking them. We didn't know that our opponents were watching us from a second-floor window. They were watching us train. We started banging the pads. We were doing a lot of kicks in preparation for the fights. *Bam, bam, bam!* My guys were hitting the pads hard from all angles at the legs.

At the weigh-in, I was told that the fight would be under full-contact rules. I started arguing, "No, this is a WKA-sanctioned fight. Kicks to the legs are allowed, and you can kick above the waist." My words fell on deaf ears. I couldn't change the full-contact rules.

When I informed my team, none of the guys wanted to fight. "We've been training for leg kicks," they said. "We've been working our asses off for this tournament. If we go to Europe, are they going to say the same thing?"

I told them, "I don't know. But we're here and have to fight by their rules." I suspected the Miami fighters saw us hitting

THE NEXT GENERATION

the pads so fucking hard that they got scared. The promoter changed the rules to protect them. A full-contact tournament gave them the advantage. In full contact, you had to kick a minimum of eight times above the waist. If you kicked less than eight times, the following round, you had to make up the difference. For example, say you only kick six times to the side or head, then you would have to kick 10 times the following round or risk disqualification.

Johnny Zea was in the first fight. It was a five-round fight. By the fourth round, he was out of gas and couldn't continue. He was telling me, "I ain't got nothing left. The airplane flight took all my energy." Johnny was a good fighter. He had all the skills and talent, but not this day. I'd seen him worn out before, and against tougher opponents, and he'd win. But not on this day.

I was pissed off and responded, "Hey cabrón (asshole), I'd rather you go out there and get knocked out than quit on this stool." It didn't matter what I said, though; he just shook his head. You can say all you want, but if a fighter gives up there is nothing more you can do. I had to tell the referee he was done. He quit on the stool. It was considered a technical knockout. You know the saying, "You can lead a horse to water but can't make them drink."

The next fight was with Miguel Reyes. He had fought full contact before in karate tournaments. The other guy was a little bigger than him. This time the fight went the distance, but the judges gave it to his opponent. I think they stole the fight from him. He had cleaner punches and kicks. The fight should have been a draw or a win for Miguel.

Now we had only David Morrow left to fight. I told him, "David if you win, we go to Europe to fight. So don't blow it!" Prior to the tournament, I had been working with David on his leg kicks. His taekwondo background focused on the upper body, so he needed to develop quicker ankle, shin, and thigh strikes for kickboxing. Even though the promoter had changed the rules to full contact, I believed it gave David an advantage for kicking to the upper body.

In kickboxing, David's signature move at the bell was to charge across the ring and immediately kick to the leg. At the start of this fight, the other guy got in a really wide stance. When the bell rang, David immediately ran across the ring and kicked him in the leg. The guy fell down and started rolling around, screaming. The referee took a point away from David.

Before the second round started, I remind him, "David you're winning this fucking fight. We got a couple of more rounds to go, and then to Europe." The bell rang and the other guy went out there and got in that wide stance again, like he was saying, "Go ahead, kick me." And David did just that. He kicked him straight to the knee. The guy fell and started screaming, "He broke my leg, he broke my leg!" I knew David had hurt him badly. There was damage to his knee. The referee stopped the fight and immediately disqualified David. So, I jumped in the ring and took off David's gloves. Some other guy jumped in the ring to pick up the gloves but pushed David's head, calling him a cheater. David immediately retaliated and hit the guy. I saw another guy going at David, so I hit him. I yelled out, "Get the fuck away from us." Security people were in the ring, and after a lot of pushing and shoving, the promoter calmed everyone down.

My team finally got back to the training room. I looked at David "That guy was an easy fight, man."

David had his head down, "Yeah, I know, but he stuck his leg out there and it was so tempting."

"It doesn't matter. Now we aren't going to Europe. My hope was for all of us or at least one of us to win."

About that time, a Cubano came into the room and approached me, saying, "Hey homie, you got problems with these gabachos (White guys)?"

I told him, "Naw, man, everything is cool. We're all right."

Shaking his head, he said, "Naw, naw, naw, everything is not cool. We seen what happened, hombre. I'll take care of it." He got on the phone, and I could hear him telling somebody, "Oye, tell the vatos…"

After we showered and dressed, we walked outside and saw three carloads of guys, all of them armed. The Cubano and the driver of one of the cars jumped out, one holding a knife and the other a machete. They were ready for war. I had to get in the middle of it and tell them. "No, no, everything is cool. What happened in the ring stays there."

Yeah, but these guys said they're gonna jump you and fuck you guys up. You were outnumbered, but not anymore." I looked at the Cubano and said, "They're not gonna do shit. Their bark is worse than their bite." The Cubano reluctantly agreed. He probably wanted to fight more than the gabachos did. We ended up at a nightclub, partying with the locals.

I couldn't help myself, I had to tell my team what I thought about the tournament. Everyone was drinking and enjoying the evening. I approached David and Johnny who probably knew they would get an earful from me at some point in the evening. I didn't disappoint them. I told David, "David, you could have beat this guy easy. He was like a sparring partner for you." He nodded his head in agreement. Then I turned to Johnny. "You're a big pussy. I've seen you beat better guys than that. You've been in worse shape, but you still won."

During the trip, David had seen a pretty waitress at a restaurant he wanted to meet. He didn't speak Spanish, so he asked me, "Hey Coach, tell me something that I can say to her when she returns with our drinks. I don't want to just say, you're pretty or good-looking. I know all the Spanish cuss words, but I can't hook up with her like that. What can I tell her to get her attention and let her know I'm interested in her?"

I said, "No problem. Tell her 'Mas chile.' She'll know what that means. I guess I was being a little chicken shit, still frustrated about my team losing.

"Thanks, Coach." As soon as the waitress returned to our table. David tried to be a Romeo, touching her arm and whispering, "mas chile." She smiled and nodded and returned with salsa that she served directly on his food. He said it a few more times, and each time she served more salsa on his food. He didn't eat chile, but on this day he did. He was sweating through his meal but happy to have had her attention. I think he eventually figured out what I had done.

I saw them soon after, sharing a drink at the bar. It was a great memory of him, enjoying life. David passed away a few years later. He took a motorcycle trip to Las Vegas with one of his fighters he had trained. On the way home he was involved in a motorcycle accident that killed him instantly.

THE NEXT GENERATION

L-R: Cuauhtémoc "Cobra" Urzua, Ernie "Lightning" Bonilla, Lorenzo "Coach" Rodriguez, Scott "Thunder" Thorson, Javier "Guacho" Diaz, and Johnny "Z" Zea.

SCOTT THORSON

Scott was considered a people's champion. He was a fighter with no background in boxing or martial arts when I first met him. At the time, I had no knowledge of him other than my observation that he was a cocky, arrogant, and selfish young man of about 19 years of age. I found out later that he, in fact, had a tough life as a child and teenager, which affected much of the good and bad he did in the intervening years.

As a child, he lived with his mother and stepfather. He believed his stepfather was his real father. He had little nurturing from his parents and soon developed emotional problems. He was placed in a behavioral health hospital for emotionally disturbed children. His mother had reached out to his birth father for help. His father introduced himself to Scott during his stay in the hospital. Tragically, while Scott was in the hospital, his stepfather murdered his mother and committed suicide.

Scott was informed of the horrible news by his birth father, who received guardianship and moved him to Riverside, California. But Scott's behavior was becoming more bizarre. Eventually, his father had to have him placed in an institution for mental health treatment. While institutionalized, he grew taller and stronger from weightlifting and exercise. When he was released from the rehabilitation center, his father enrolled him in high school. Scott had become stronger and popular with girls, but continued his use of drugs and alcohol. His violent temper became worse each passing day.

In 1989–1990, his best friend, Josh, was on his way to a gym to practice kickboxing and invited Scott to train. Josh introduced Scott to my student, David Morrow. Josh realized that Scott needed to find a way to release all his anger and thought training in kickboxing would help. Scott only agreed to go with Josh because he was bored. He didn't think anything would come of it.

He liked the kickboxing class. He said many times about kickboxing, "I could put on boxing gloves and punch somebody in the face and not go to jail for it. I loved it." He became exhilarated hitting the big bag. He said every time he hit the bag, "I felt this sudden release of anger and frustration. The more I hit the bag, the better I felt. The harder I hit the bag, the more peace I found inside me. I was hooked and wanted more. I was so full of hate and anger over what my stepfather did to my mom."

David Morrow brought Scott to the El Monte school. I was conducting a smoker event at the time. With no fighting experience, Scott without hesitation went in the ring to fight against a much more experienced fighter. No one gave him a chance. Especially me. I was ready to stop the fight if it looked like he was gonna get hurt. It was five one-minute rounds.

Scott was taking a beating. He blocked most of the punches with his face, but he would not back down. It was like he wanted to get hit, he wanted to feel the pain. I was impressed at his courage, but not his fighting skills. He had no kickboxing skills at that point in his life. But he had plenty of rage. Surprisingly, in the fourth round, Scott broke the leg of his opponent and won the fight. Scott just stood over the guy and laughed at him.

After about six months of intensive training, I took a group of fighters to Bakersfield to compete in a tournament promoted by Abe Belardo. Scott was one of my fighters. As happens often, the main event challenger didn't show up. Neither did Scott's opponent in a lower card match up. Abe approached me about having Scott fight the main event for the California State Super Lightweight Championship.

I asked him. "Scotty, do you think you're ready? Do you want to fight for the state championship?" Scott nodded, and I let him take the fight. He knocked out the fighter in the fourth round. A month or so later, I sat down with Scott and David Morrow and said, "Scott, I got something for you" and pulled out the state championship belt he had won.

I told him, "I'm not going to give it to you unless you agree that this is what you want to do. Was this fight just a fly-by-night thing and you just got lucky? Or do you want to get better and commit yourself to fighting?"

Scott agreed he was lucky, but he wanted to fight again. I told him, "If you want to fight for me, then you will have to live with me under my roof. You can't use drugs, smoke, or alcohol; and you must respect my rules and my wife's rules, and train six days a week." Scott eagerly agreed. If I had known about his mental health concerns at the time, I'm not sure if I would have invited him to stay with me. I have no doubt Scott had a guardian angel looking over his shoulder that brought him to me.

The more I trained Scott, the more I realized he had a Clark Kent/Superman dual personality. He would literally change into a super fighting beast when he'd get in the ring. I'd wake him each day at 4:30 or 5:00 a.m. to start his five-mile run before he went to work. Then he'd have to drive in L.A. traffic to get to my El Monte school to train in the evening. He was notoriously bad in the training room. He would go through the motions on the bags, and his sparring sessions were comical. He'd take more punches and kicks than he delivered. But his daily running regime saved him from getting fatigued during fights.

Scott's fights were so action packed that, even if he lost, the fight was considered to be the fight of the night. Scott was a beast and never backed down when he fought. During his first fight with me as his trainer, Scott fought Johnny Zaya. Johnny Zaya was a good fighter who had knocked out Danny Steele, a great fighter in his day. Scott was winning the fight but taking hit after hit to the face, telling Johnny, "Come on hit me, you can't hurt me."

After the third round was over, I jumped in the ring and started scolding him. "Keep your hands up—don't let him use your face as a punching bag!"

Suddenly, Scott grabbed my face and kissed me on the forehead and said, "I love you, Papa." I didn't know what to say. I looked at him, a bit shocked, and said, "Just keep your hands up!"

This was Scott's first five-round fight under me. He dominated the fight and won by unanimous decision. I was proud of him.

Audiences got their money's worth when Scott battled in the ring. His penchant for ignoring the shots to his face and body and fearlessly standing toe to toe with his opponent made him a fan favorite. Scott earned a commission on tickets that he sold for fight events. He eagerly went about making ticket sales a priority. He averaged 300 hundred to 600 ticket sales each time he fought. He was by far the most popular fighter I ever trained.

I had been fortunate to promote some of Scott's best fights. I took him and some fighters to a tournament called USA vs. Russia. It was held at the Irving Bren Event Center. Scott's fighter didn't show up, and there was a Russian fighter whose opponent didn't show either. Scott wanted to fight him, but I told him, "No, Scotty, he's a professional. He's out of your league." Scott was still an amateur.

Scott was adamant about fighting. He had sold a lot of tickets for the fight and wanted to put on a show for his fans. I don't know why, but I gave into him. He was determined to fight that day. Scott fought Sylvester Maubush, who was taller with a great reach advantage. As I had predicted, Sylvester bloodied Scott up. Scott was no match for the Russian. It didn't matter, though; Scott kept getting up off the floor yelling at Maubush, "Come on, hit me again." And Maubush did exactly that, repeatedly. The fight went the distance and Scott lost the decision. The crowd loved the fight. You could see Scott's popularity grow, even in a loss. Karate champion and celebrated actor Chuck Norris was in attendance and came up to Scott, shaking his hand, congratulating him on having a great fight.

As Scott was going back to the trainer's room to get stitched up, this man approached him. "Man, that was the most amazing fight I have ever seen." He handed him a business card that read "Michael Berk, Producer." Berk asked Scott if he would consider doing some fight scenes with the *Baywatch* TV series. I thought it was a great opportunity for him. We agreed to go.

When Scott arrived at the studio, the casting agent asked him to read some lines. Scott read the lines and she looked over at Berk and said, "We found our Steve Thorn." Thorn was a character in one of the *Baywatch* episodes who was a kickboxer. Berk hired Scott for an episode of *Baywatch* called "Kicks."

I had secured a contract for Scott's life story called, "Latin Roots, American Thunder." Berk, one of the producers for *Baywatch*, was interested. Berk even talked about getting Edward Olmos to play me as Scott's trainer. I found out later that Berk told Scott, "Look, let us write it and produce it for you. If I can do your life story, then I'll see if we can keep you on the show."

He paid Scott $2,000 for the rights to the movie project. Ultimately, Berk got into a disagreement with Scott and some others we had spoken with about the project. Berk backed out of our project and Scott only had that one *Baywatch* appearance. The "Latin Roots, American Thunder," story got shelved. Scott blamed himself for losing the movie opportunity.

After the *Baywatch* episode, Scott had a commitment for another title fight but instead wanted to go Las Vegas to celebrate his 21st birthday. I reminded him of his fight obligation and told him if he went to Vegas and didn't train with me, he could not return to my home. Scott chose to go to Vegas, where he eventually slipped back to alcohol and drug addiction.

I lost communication with him for a few years. But whenever he needed money, he would call me, hoping I could get him a fight. I told him if he was serious about training, he'd have to clean up, stop drinking and using drugs. These calls occurred a few times over the year. Scott couldn't or wouldn't commit. It was sad. He was married with two daughters but was back on methamphetamine, weed, and alcohol binges.

A few years later, Scott got clean and sober and was fighting for the USKO karate gym. He competed in one of my promotional tournaments. He was out of shape and lost badly. I spoke

THE NEXT GENERATION

with him and asked, "Scotty, what happened to you? You're better than this." I knew it was his addictions that betrayed him.

Sometime later, I saw Scott fight at another of my promotional tournaments. He was fighting Rob McCullum for the United States Kickboxing Welterweight Championship. He had lost the first two rounds badly. I was frustrated at him and the trainer. I jumped in the ring before the start of the third round and told the trainer, "Get out of the ring!"

I looked at Scott and told him, "You got this guy. Just do what I tell you." I told him what to do to counter McCullum. He won the last three rounds and won the fight by split decision. He later fought McCullum again and lost to him by split decision. They were both great fights.

I trained Scott for two more fights. His last fight was a pay-per-view event. Scott knocked the guy out with a kick to the head. I told him after the fight, "Scotty, we're done. Go out on top. Go out with a win and this good memory." Scott agreed and ended his kickboxing career. He was in his mid-30s.

Scott and I remain friends and have kept in touch over the years. He has fully recovered from his drug and alcohol use and found faith in Jesus Christ. His faith saved his life. He is happily living with his wife and children in Tennessee. He earned a bachelor's degree in social work and currently works with abused women as a domestic violence crisis response manager. He chronicled his life story in a book called *Empty Spaces*, a heartfelt story of his victory over addiction. He remains a staunch supporter for therapeutic addiction intervention and is an active public speaker in the community. He retired from kickboxing as a former Super Lightweight and Welterweight champion, winning the California State Championship, the North American Championship, and the United States Championship during his fight career.

THE PELENQUE

I was fortunate to have taken teams to Minnesota. We won some of those battles and lost others, which is normal in tournament fighting. I also took teams to Hawaii and Canada on a number of occasions. Scott Thorson beat the champion in Hawaii. He also fought Miguel Reyes twice, once in Tijuana and another time in Los Angeles. Scott won both times.

I took a real great team to Mexico in the early '90s. The fight was sanctioned by the Sports Commission under the federal government of Mexico. The Mexican Tourist Department sponsored the tournament. They were trying to promote more tourism from the United States into Mexico. We were going to fight at the Pelenque in Tijuana.

The Pelenque was where they held concerts, bullfights, and cockfights. It was a great arena because the ring sat below the audience. When we went to sign the contract, the promoter gave each of us a token "Key to the City." They took us to meet sponsors at a couple of nightclubs to promote the show. Every time we met a sponsor, they would serve us a round of "slammers," watered-down alcohol shots. The next day, everyone had the chorros (diarrhea). It was a shitty morning.

I rented a van and took my "Chorro Team" to fight. The team included James Saldaña, a heavyweight. He fought Miguel's student, Pedro "The Pitbull" Fernandez. My student, Jesse Cervantes, fought Juan "Cyclone" Serna for the welterweight title. Miguel fought Scott Thorson for the lightweight title. And I took on Gus Martinez, who fought flyweight. The Pelenque held a large and noisy crowd. We were excited to fight.

James lost the heavyweight fight from a spinning back knuckle. I thought Pedro's elbow connected, which is considered an illegal strike. I protested, but to no avail. Regardless, it was a great fight; it had gone four rounds before the questionable hit. The fight was stopped on a cut, and Pitbull was awarded the win for the heavyweight title. Jesse won his fight against Cyclone. Scott beat Miguel by decision. And Gus lost to me by decision. I was proud of our performance. Every fighter on both teams gave his best effort and got the best in return. Overall, the Pelenque Tournament was a great experience.

6
MIXED MARTIAL ARTS

A DIFFERENT FIGHT JOURNEY

I HAD TO CLOSE THE El Monte Self Defense School sometime during the late '90s. Money and family issues forced my decision. I figured it was time to hang up my gloves and just focus on work and family obligations. My backyard was full of my gym equipment and two boxing rings that were not set up. I was ready to move on from professional fighting. Something was telling me to hang up the gloves and just work a regular job. The martial arts were my first love, and I thought I was ready to let it go. But the fighting arts weren't done with me just yet.

I lived in Moreno Valley, a sprawling desert valley in southern California. Without traffic, it was about a 40-minute drive away from Los Angeles. I was working in Pest Control at night and would get home around 6:00 a.m. One of my former El Monte students, Carlos Gonzales, would show up at my house after working graveyard as a truck driver in Ontario. He'd nap in his car, waiting for me to get home.

Carlos wanted me to train him in kickboxing. He was committed and had a fighter's heart. I attended high school with his father. His grandfather had brought him to me at my El Monte school to teach him boxing as a young kid to keep him off the streets. In the barrios, most parents had the same reasons for introducing their children to sports or martial arts. They were willing to spend their hard-earned money for their children. But only a few remained committed to train as they got older. Carlos was now an adult and committed to the fight game.

Upon arriving home from work, I found him asleep in his car. I'd wake him up and tell him to go home. He'd get out of his car and try to convince me to train him. In my mind, since I had closed my school, I had retired from the fight game. But Carlos wouldn't take no for an answer. He just kept on coming over to my house. Finally, after a few weeks of his nagging, I agreed.

I told him, "All right. If we do this, then we have to do it right." We cleaned out my garage and set up the gym for training.

I started working with him in circuit training with punching and kicking drills. He got better each week. After about six months, I took him to David Morrow's martial art school in Moreno Valley, where he could spar. David introduced me to Brian Foster, a heavyweight MMA fighter. David was Brian's MMA trainer.

Carlos and I went to David's school to spar in boxing and kickboxing only. At first, Brian could weave his body and duck away from Carlos easily in the ring. He'd counter with shots to Carlos's head. Carlos had a hard head and wouldn't back down. These were great training experiences for him. Eventually, Carlos overcame Brian's defense and started dominating the sparring sessions. Carlos would frustrate Brian so much that Brian would try and wrestle Carlos to the ground. Brian knew Carlos had improved as a fighter.

I noticed Brian would do whatever he felt like doing as far as training was concerned. He had no set training regime. As a rule, I kept all my students on a strict training schedule and regime. I expected all my students to be champions in the streets or on the mat. Carlos was no different. When David closed his school, Brian came to my home and asked me to be his trainer.

TEAM QUEST

When Brian first came to train with me, he held the Heavyweight title. He defeated Frank Rodriguez by submission (strikes) in the first round of the 1999 Bas Rutten King-of-the-Cage Tournament at the Soboba Casino in southern California. Brian knew I had made Carlos a better fighter as his trainer. He wanted me to do the same for him.

I told him, "If I train you, you're not going to train like you did at David's school. You're going to have to do everything I tell you to do." He happily agreed.

I began training both Carlos and Brian in my garage. Brian always mentioned that his goal was to make Dan Henderson's MMA Team. Dan trained his team regularly in Temecula, not far from my house. After some time, I told Brian, "Let's go see what this guy Henderson has at his school."

Brian took me to a high school in Temecula. I guess the school wasn't charging Henderson for space because of his notoriety as an Olympic competitor. I learned that Dan Henderson was a celebrated Greco Roman wrestler, holding the national championship at the senior level in 1993, 1994, and 1997. He also represented the United States in the 1992 and 1996 Summer Olympics but didn't win any medals.

Brian took me to the high school, and I watched as Henderson's MMA students began arriving. They didn't warm up; no stretching, only bullshitting with each other. They put their gear on and did whatever they wanted to do. No training regime just random, half-assed efforts on the equipment.

I thought to myself, "Wow, these guys are supposed to be top-notch MMA fighters? These guys are pro fighters?"

It wasn't the fault of the fighters. I recognized that MMA had just arrived on the national scene as an American fighting sport. A lot of the events were illegal, with no sanctioning commission oversight. Some promoters would set up events and walk away with the sponsorship entry fees of the fighters. Many of the fights were not ranked by experience, resulting in shameful mismatches. Amateurs would be matched with pros.

Those poor guys would get beat badly or worse, injured. All the fighters had heart, but many had no skills for the ring They were underground fights, held on military bases, in Mexico border fights, at private club venues, or on the Indian reservations. Sometimes, the fighters didn't get paid for fighting. Promoters would take the money and disappear. It was the wild, wild west of fighting sports.

This was the world Brian and other promising fighters wanted to be in, the MMA. Brian and I would go to the high school about two or three times a week. Brian used to get spanked when he sparred with the other fighters, but soon his fighting skills improved. They couldn't hit him, and he'd retaliate with counterpunches and kicks, beating them soundly. They knew he was training with someone. They asked him about me. That was why he had invited me to go check out the training.

I saw guys getting hurt, not warming up and training without proper hand wraps or gloves. New fighters would show up and want to spar but didn't have proper equipment. It didn't take long before I took over the training sessions.

I've never been the type of person to sit back and wait for others to do the right thing, especially when it came to training. I brought them proper equipment and began organizing the training and sparring regime. When Dan was no longer able to use the high school, he started coming to my house for training. Eventually, others and I convinced Dan to open a school. Dan soon found a place in Temecula, California, naming it Team Quest.

EL PACHUCO

I met Art "Pachuco" Santore at Dan Henderson's school. He took the name Pachuco because a relative had been in the popular *El Pachuco* theatre play by Luis Valdez that starred Edward Olmos as the Pachuco character. Art told me that before I was Brian's trainer, he could hit him easily. But Brian had such a hard head, he would just walk through it. After a while, Art couldn't hit him anymore. Brian had advanced in his fighting techniques. That was when Art decided to come to my house. He wanted me to train him too.

Dan, Art, and Brian were all former wrestlers. They had no stand-up training in boxing or kickboxing. They were training in MMA, the ground-and-pound techniques, but lacked the stand-up skills and conditioning for ring fighting. I was showing them techniques of Thai boxing and kickboxing.

L-R: Art "Pachuco" Santore and his wife; MMA fighter Randy Couture; and Lorenzo "Coach" Rodriguez, circa 2002.

They were very respectful of me as their trainer. Because of my age and background, they readily accepted everything I demanded of them as a trainer. I have no doubt they checked into my fight history. I have always trained champions like a fighter and fighters like a champion. They knew I was providing skills that were new to them as fighters but critical for becoming champions in the ring.

MMA was still a young fight game. At the time, the UFC was in the process of purchasing the rights to PRIDE. PRIDE Fighting Championships was a Japanese mixed martial arts promotion company. There was a lot of fraud and brutally unfair fights occurring within the MMA fighting organizations. Art had tried out for the UFC. He went to one of those so-called open recruitment tryouts but didn't make the cut. In my opinion, those events were scams. You'd pay around $200 to try out, but most of the guys never got picked up. The promoters usually knew who they wanted. Only the best of the rest (Pride,

King-of-the-Cage, Strike Force and Bellator, etc.) would get a call to join the UFC. El Pachuco never made it to the UFC but remained a top MMA fighter with me as his trainer. From 2001 to 2009, Art won title bouts in King-of-the-Cage, World Extreme Fighting, Total Combat, and the Gladiator Challenge.

JOE SARKISSIAN

I became the main trainer at Team Quest. Initially, Team Quest only wanted students 16 years and older. I encouraged Dan to recruit kids to Team Quest and not focus merely on training fighters for tournaments. The money and future were in training youth. Fighters are not the future for a school. They come and go. But parents would pay to keep their children in classes, especially if they saw a positive change in their behavior because of it.

I took Joe Sarkissian, one of my fighters, to help train at Team Quest. Team Quest wanted to start an aerobic kickboxing class and have me lead it. I told them, "I didn't come to teach aerobics, I came to train fighters. If I'm not going to do that, then I'm not going to stay here." I would train the morning class. And then, the Team Quest class. In the afternoon, I'd start the children's class. I was fortunate to convince Team Quest to have Joe teach the conditioning class. He was busy training for another championship belt and could use the gas money. When I left, Team Quest hired him as their primary trainer. Joe had an interesting fight history that made him a good choice to be the lead trainer.

When Joe was 15, a red-headed ball of energy, he went with me and David Morrow to watch a kickboxing event in Tijuana on August 18, 2006. We went a day early to avoid the traffic at the border and enjoy the night life. All the guys drank heavy that night except me and David. David was supposed to fight a guy the following month. The following day, David weighed-in, signed the contract, and was to be introduced at the show that evening to promote the US vs. Mexico fight for next month.

As it happened, they needed one more fighter for the card that night or they would have to cancel the show. This was not unusual in the fight game. When a fighter gets injured or is unavailable, the promoter is tasked to find an immediate replacement or possibly cancel the whole event at a loss, if the contract specified a set number of fights on the card. Miguel Reyes' brother was the promoter. In a rush, he pleaded with David and me to have one of our fighters fill the vacant spot to avoid the canceling the event. He failed to mention that it would be a title fight, a five-round fight.

The guy that I thought could take the fight was Victor Martinez, but he didn't want it. He may have been hung over or not mentally ready to jump in the ring cold. Victor was tall, in great shape, and a better boxer than Joe. Instead, Joe was begging to take the fight. David was his trainer. I asked David, "Is he ready?" Joe, 15 years foolish, was all game. "I'll fight, I'll fight." So David relented and said okay. We had to borrow equipment for him to fight, and I gave him a B-12 vitamin shot before he went in the ring. We had partied late into the evening the night before, and I knew he'd tire quickly.

I told the promoter, "We'll take the fight, but he can only go three rounds. I don't even know if he can make the three rounds." It wasn't part of our plan to fight at all. We had been partying the night before, no one imagined we'd be asked to fight the next day.

But the promoter kept pleading with me. "Lorenzo, I just need one more fighter. If I can't get someone, I'll have to cancel everything."

Only because Joe was gung-ho about fighting, David and I reluctantly agreed. But I told the promoter, "He can only fight three rounds."

The promoter told me, "That's okay, it doesn't matter how many rounds it goes, as long as I have the fight on the schedule."

So when it was Joe's turn to fight, he entered the ring and the announcer told the crowd, "This is a five-round kickboxing championship fight." I yelled out to the promoter, "Hey, I said only three rounds!" But he looked up at me, shrugging his shoulders, and said, "I didn't tell them to announce that." I knew he was bullshitting me because I had just learned from the announcer it was a championship fight. He would be fighting the reigning champion, Sergio "Salvavidas" (The Lifeguard) Garcia for the MMX Super Welterweight Muay Thai Kickboxing World Championship title.

In the first round, Joe represented himself well, but he came back to the corner sucking air. The champ had already methodically figured out Joe's tendencies and hammered away at his body. Joe was already tired. I told him, "That's okay, just tie him up, give yourself time to get your second wind." Joe went out in the second round and instead of holding off the champion by dancing around the ring, pushing off or holding him, he wrestled the champ to the floor. The crowd started booing, and the referee gave him and the corner a warning. The third round started and instead of tying him up, Joe took the champion to the ground again. The crowd was angry and booing us more loudly. I don't blame the crowd; we had no business taking the fight.

When the round ended, Joe was exhausted, and I knew he couldn't continue without getting hurt. I called the fight off, and the champion got credit for a knockout. The promoter told me we wouldn't get paid because Joe quit. I reminded him that I had agreed to only three rounds. He said, "Yeah, but I thought I'd get my five rounds once he was in the ring."

The promoter didn't want to pay me. So I told him, "If you don't pay me, you and I are going to have some fun." He knew who I was and exactly what I meant. He decided to pay us. I got $200 for Joe and $100 each for David and me.

Years went by, and I was now Joe's trainer and saw him maturing as a kickboxer. He had already won the US Amateur Champion belt when he decided to join the Marines. I told him, "You better come back. When you do, I will make you a champion. Just come back."

Joe served his country during wartime in Iraq and, as promised, returned home unharmed. As I promised, I got him a fight at the Hollywood Park Casino. He was fighting for the California Welterweight title. He beat the guy in the first round. Only a minute passed in the fight. I told him, "Look, that was too easy. We've been training so hard. Let me make some phone calls. Don't party! I want to get you another fight as soon as possible."

Luckily, there was a fight the following week in Tijuana. It was a championship fight. I told the promoter that Joe would put his belt up against the champion's belt. Once I was sure how much he'd get paid, we agreed to the fight. His opponent was Sergio "Salvavidas" Garcia—the same man he fought 15 years prior, at the age of 15.

Joe put an ass-kicking on Salvavidas, winning a unanimous decision. He not only took the belt, he retired him. After the decision, Salvavidas took the microphone from the ring announcer and told the crowd in Spanish, "I fought this guy when he was a kid, and now all these years later, it comes full circle. I fight him again, and he beats me. I don't mind giving the belt to the guy that beat me." Salvavidas retired from kickboxing following the defeat.

Joe became the head trainer at Team Quest. They would let me train him there, but he could not represent me as a member of Rodriguez Kickboxing at any tournament or title fights. But he still wanted me to be his trainer. I reminded him that I don't get paid if he fights for Team Quest, so it didn't benefit me to continue training him. He understood. He trained Dan Henderson in his 2007 title fight against Quinton "Rampage" Jackson for the Light Heavyweight unification title between the Pride and UFC belts. But Joe wasn't invited on the team flight to London, England. Dan lost on decision to Jackson, and Joe never got paid as Dan's trainer.

Joe decided to quit as a trainer for Team Quest but continued to fight as a kickboxer. He had four fights and lost all of them, two of them by knockout. He came back to me, wanting me to be his trainer. I was reluctant to take him back because he fought for Team Quest and another trainer. I questioned his loyalty. "I took you to Team Quest and helped make you a better fighter. But you chose them over me. How do I know you won't do it again?" He had no response; he knew what he had done wasn't fair to me. But fighters are like your children. They will disappoint you, but you always take them back.

I started training him again. I took him to the Commerce Casino, where he fought a Japanese guy and knocked him out in the second round. I took him to Canada to fight and to the Riverside Convention Center, where he fought as a junior welterweight. He won the IKKC Muay Thai Welterweight California Championship fight at the San Bernardino Fairgrounds in Victorville.

He stopped fighting because promoters weren't providing a fair amount for the fighter or trainers. The pay didn't even cover the training and equipment costs. Fair compensation was a constant battle for fighters in kickboxing and boxing. And Joe was getting too old for the ring. Joe wisely decided to retire. All fighters do; some learn sooner than later.

CUTMAN

During my time as a trainer, I was getting 15 percent of whatever the fighter got paid. If I took a few fighters for an event, I got a good paycheck for the night. It didn't happen on a regular basis, so I had to look for other ways to make money. With the advent of MMA, I soon became a professional cutman. There weren't enough skilled cornermen to handle cuts during a fight. Likewise, guys were getting injured from poor wraps on their hands and wrists. Some guys were putting gloves on without any wraps—a sure way to injure a wrist or break fingers.

A cutman is responsible for preventing and treating physical damage to a fighter during the breaks between rounds of a full-contact match in boxing, kickboxing, or an MMA bout. Cutmen typically handle swelling, nosebleeds, and lacerations. Cutmen might also tape fighters' hands, which helps protect the bones and tendons. The term "wrap" is commonly used to describe the method of using gauze and tape on fighters' hands and wrists.

UFC usually hired two guys as cutmen for the blue and red corners. Some promoters at smaller venues would contact cutmen to sell their services to trainers. I didn't like to do that because trainers, if they don't know you, are suspicious. You may be working for the other side and wrapping hands poorly on purpose. When I went to the Gladiators Challenge, the promoter wanted me to go around and see who needed a wrap. I didn't like to do it because some trainers are offended, believing you think they don't know how to wrap. From my experience, it was true; many didn't know how to wrap properly. Their fighters would get injured, and the promoter would be on the hook to pay the insurance for his medical needs. It's always best to have a professional cutman do that work.

One time at a Twentynine Palms casino event, they wouldn't let the other cornerman work. He had some tickets or some legal issue that prevented him from entering the event. The promoter asked me to work both corners. Whoever was cut the worse was the fighter I worked on. I unwisely agreed, it wasn't fair. I was spending maybe 30 seconds in one corner and running to the other side to work. Both corners deserved equal attention by the cutman. I asked the promoter, "Am I getting paid for both corners?" Of course, the answer was no. When I promoted a fight, I always provide gauze and tape to the fighters. That way I knew they had the right material. If the corners needed wrapping services, I would offer my stepson or someone I had trained.

I had three guys fighting at a Victorville event. None of my guys needed cuts worked on, and I had already prepared the tincture for cuts. I asked a trainer if they needed a cutman. The solution was prepared and still fresh for fights. The trainer looks at me and said, "Naw, my guy never gets cut. He'll be all right."

The first round, the fighter got cut with a spinning elbow. It opened up a big gash over his eyebrow. I could see the trainer looking for me, but I had already thrown away the solution. He found me and asked me to work the corner. I told him I had already thrown away the tincture, and if I mixed a new batch, I'd have to charge him double. But it didn't matter; the referee stopped the fight because of the cut.

I had become an expert cutman for boxing, kickboxing, and MMA. Some guys I taught to wrap eventually became professional cutmen too. The wraps are all different. Boxing and kickboxing are similar, but some states actually measure the tape amount. In unsanctioned fights, some trainers were making casts around the hand. It was like swinging with cement fists. You could lose a fight if the wrap is too tight or too loose; the fighter's hand could be injured. Likewise, if you are working on a cut to close it, applying too much pressure could open the wound even deeper. It takes longer to heal, and the fighter can't train or take another fight. It's an art to be a good cutman.

EL PADRE DE LIMALAMA, MEXICO

LimaLama may not have survived and thrived if it hadn't been for Grandmaster (GM) Rigoberto "Rigo" Lopez. For that reason, he is considered by many Latino martial artists as the Father of LimaLama in Mexico and Latino America.

He was born in Morelia, Michoacán, in 1946. As a young man, Rigo became infatuated with physical fitness training, which led to his eventually winning the Bodybuilding title of "Mr. Michoacán." He moved to Tampico, Tamaulipas, to work at "Los Fabulosos" gym and met his future wife, Maria Griselda Orta Guzmán. There he earnestly began studying martial arts and raising a family.

He arrived in Tijuana in 1964 and worked at the Eduardo "Mr. Universo" Silvestre Gymnasium. In 1966, Rigo earned a black belt in Okinawa Shōrin-Ryū under Master Fernando Ruiz of Puerto Rico. That same year, he received a brown belt in judo under Master Fernando Betancourt of Tijuana, Mexico. During this period, Rigo had already begun competing in karate tournaments in different areas of Mexico, Central America, and the United States.

He consistently finished at the top levels in Kumite and Katas. But that didn't keep him from continuing his bodybuilding passion. In 1967, Rigo won the "Mister Baja California" Bodybuilding title. From there, Rigo represented Baja California in the competition for the "Mr. Mexico" title, where he came in 3rd place.

Grandmaster Rigoberto Lopez, circa 1967.

LimaLama Masters Richard Nuñez and Sal Esquivel are credited for introducing Master Rigoberto Lopez to GM Tino during the mid-1960s. Master Rigo was fascinated with the fluid power of LimaLama. He knew that Masters Sal and Richard were accomplished martial arts fighters trained in Kajukenbo, a merciless martial art style created in Hawaii. Yet, when Rigo watched GM Tino spar, his skill level of fighting was beyond anything Rigo seen before. The fluidity of Tino's movements, the speed of the hands, and the ferocious whipping palm strikes to all parts of the body had Rigo in awe. That is what eventually brought him under the tutelage of GM Tino, wanting to master this new martial art called LimaLama.

In the early 1970s, as a young man, I first saw Rigo fight at a Long Beach karate tournament. He was in exceptional shape and strong as a burro. But what impressed me the most was that he moved like a jaguar. He was agile, quick, and fluid in his hand and feet movements. He had already mastered LimaLama.

GM Rigo is credited with establishing a standardized system and curriculum for LimaLama belt promotions. It wasn't easy, because GM Tino had always trained black belts and brown belts based on what he thought they could understand or grasp. He had no patience for slow learners. GM Tino assumed that a black belt should be able to pick up whatever form he showed them. There was no structured pattern to his training. He gave you what he thought was important at that moment. GM Tino would show you a form. Once he thought you understood, he would then show you three or four different variations based on the same technique.

GM Rigo is credited as the first person to put LimaLama techniques in an order based on the belt ranking system. To my knowledge, it had never been done before. During the mid-1960s, GM Rigo would take a student with him when he visited GM Tino for training. Rigo would have his student practice the move with GM Tino while he took notes. He did this for almost two years, traveling between Tijuana and Los Angeles.

GM Tino and his sons Rudy and Myron, along with Masters Sal Esquivel and Richard Nuñez, routinely visited Rigo in Tijuana, Mexico. I was fortunate to be included as part of the sparring and training events. But it is undoubtedly GM Rigoberto Lopez who gave LimaLama a home in Mexico. As a result of GM Rigo's efforts, LimaLama began to flourish in Mexico and beyond. Its value as a hybrid fighting art soon spread across the world, with an estimated 100,000 practitioners.

MIXED MARTIAL ARTS

GM Rigoberto Lopez, circa 1980/2010.

GM Rigo soon created his own hybrid martial art based on his own training in Okinawa Shōrin-Ryū, judo, LimaLama, and other karate styles. He called it *Kung Do Lama*. I may have forgotten or missed some of his original students, but here is a list of some of his first-generation students who became Masters:

Kung Do Lama, Latino America

THE 9TH DEGREE

On or about August of 2021, I got a call from Sensei Hector Ventoura. Hector was close friends with GM Rigo and wanted me to attend the LimaLama Mexican Federation event with him in Tijuana the following month. He asked, "How do you want your name spelled on the certificate?"

"What certificate?"

"We are going to honor you with a 9th degree certificate in LimaLama. GM Garza, GM Rigo, and I will be there to share the honor."

It was supposed to be a surprise, but Sensei Hector wanted to make sure about the formal spelling of my name and had no choice but to ask. I was grateful that they wanted to recognize me. But I really didn't care. I always saw myself as a fighter first. Once I got a black belt, I continued to train and expand my martial arts education but never felt I needed to tell someone about my degrees. I was happy that 'Papa,' Tino, had formally recognized my growth in LimaLama; I never introduced myself among my peers as a black belt or mentioned any degrees. I just used my birth name, Lorenzo. If someone wanted to know about my degrees, I'd prefer to demonstrate it on the mat, in the ring, or on the street.

When I received my 8th degree public recognition from GM Tino, I was grateful for Papa bestowing such an honor on me. But the degree certificate itself would cost over $900. Back in early 2000s, that was money I needed for my school rent or house payments. I couldn't afford it. In my mind, I debated the decision for a moment. I decided I really didn't need a piece of paper to prove my status. The fact that over the years GM Tino had advanced my degree belts was recognition enough.

We arrived at our hotel in Tijuana on Friday, the night before the LimaLama Federation in Mexico would conduct their meeting. Master Kiypo Tuiolosega, GM Tino's youngest son from his first wife, Claire, was expected to attend the meeting but was in the hospital undergoing treatment. He was a big Samoan. We were disappointed that he couldn't make it.

Sensei Hector advised that some of the funds raised from the karate tournament to be held that night would be donated for Kiypo's treatment. Kiypo's student, Master George Lugo, attended on his behalf, representing the Tuiolosega family. Master Lugo arrived with some of his students, two of whom would be testing the next day for their 8th and 9th degrees.

I remember the first time I met Kiypo, years ago. I was already fighting in kickboxing tournaments and had a few championship belts. I wanted to get in the ring with Myron or Rudy to spar. I knew they'd give me a good fight. Instead, they told Kiypo to spar with me. He got in the ring, thinking it would be an easy fight. It was, but not for him. I knocked him out quickly.

His older brothers had apparently set him up, knowing I wouldn't back down. Every time I'd see Kiypo, he'd always bring it up, saying, "Man, I got in the ring thinking, I'm gonna kick this little Mexican guy's ass. All of a sudden, I'm on my back waking up. Remember that time you knocked me out, Lorenzo? Man, Myron set me up. I thought I was gonna have an easy fight." That was his conversation with me. He was a good-hearted warrior. Sadly, he passed away before his prime in early 2023.

Sensei Hector Ventoura and I attended the 2021 LimaLama Mexico Federation Karate Tournament Friday evening. One of the promoters approached me and said, "They want to introduce you." As I walked to the ring, he told Sensei Hector, "They want you too, Maestro." Only minutes after they introduced us and took our picture, Sensei Hector began getting text messages condemning him for joining the Federation. We thought it was silly.

It reminded me why I took up kickboxing. I never cared for the politics in some of the martial arts schools. Loyalty to the art was one thing, but allegiance to a school was based on economics in most cases. There were fees to pay if you aligned with a school or organization. In kickboxing, I could fight for a belt without aligning with a school or particular organization. It was simple. You kick my ass, or I kick yours; regardless of the outcome, we both get paid.

On September 4, 2021, there were about 30 masters from different schools throughout Mexico. GM Rigo hosted the testing of the students and black belts. He shared the history of LimaLama in Mexico. I thought GM Al Garza, who was the first historian of LimaLama in the United States, would speak, but he didn't. It was an opportunity lost that we never got to hear. As of this writing, our friend and martial arts brother, Al Garza, is undergoing treatment for cancer.

Sensei Hector Ventoura, GM Rigoberto López and Sensei Tadashi Yamashita, circa 2015.

GM Garza, Sensei Ventoura, and Master Lugo witnessed and signed my certificate. The degree ceremony and testing were at a building close to GM Rigo's school. During the presentation, GM Rigo spoke about how long he had known me and witnessed my growth as a LimaLama fighter. As Sensei Ventoura handed me the certificate, he shared my fight history in kickboxing and Muay Thai and noted the many champions that I had trained through the years.

I was handed the microphone, and I momentarily lost my train of thought and struggled to find the right words to describe my thanks. Finally, I said, "I wish Papa Tino was here to see this group and know that LimaLama is doing well. I am grateful for this recognition, but even more grateful because now I have three fathers: my birth papa, Don Lorenzo; my LimaLama Papa, Tino; and my Mexican LimaLama Papa, Rigo. I looked directly at GM Rigo when I mentioned his name. I could see his eyes welling with tears, so I looked away to keep from losing my composure too. I was comforted, knowing that Papa Rigo knew I meant what I had said.

EPILOGUE

BLACK BELT INSTRUCTORS HAVE many titles. Master, Sifu, Sensei, Guru, Kru, and Professor or Maestro (Teacher) are the most commonly used in the different styles. I have been called all of them at one time or another. I never corrected anyone for referring to me with those labels, because it was meant as a term of respect and endearment. But I was never comfortable with the terms. The word "Master" reminded me of the era of slavery. And my students weren't slaves to me. Likewise, Maestro or Professor seemed better suited for identifying an educated man or woman. I had a high school diploma and didn't feel I had earned any scholarly distinction.

I readily admit that as a 9th degree black belt, I should be considered an expert in martial arts. But using a title before my name felt like I was putting myself above others. I am my parents' son; call me by my name, Lorenzo. When asked, I tell people my name but if they still want to show respect by using a title, I tell them, "Call me coach." A coach guides and mentors others to accomplish goals. I coached men, women, and children in martial arts, to protect themselves and those dear to them. I coached them to be their best, physically and mentally.

I coached them to be confident and purposeful inside and outside the ring. I coached them to be warriors in life.

It has been my experience that when a fighter joins a school or gym, he is considered *fresh meat* to the other fighters. They take turns pounding on him until he gives up and quits or endures the punishment. When a new fighter would join, it was that person's turn to be the meat that got pounded. By the time I became a black belt, I realized that the way I had been taught scared away potential great fighters. The old ways may have been successful for finding guys that have heart and a passion for fighting, but it didn't mean they were the best fighters in the ring or outside it.

As a coach, I believed it was best to establish conditioning and proper form first, teaching a student how to move, strike, and counter an attack. Matching students with a person at their level and weight provided a better training environment for them to grow in the art. Testing them against more seasoned fighters in controlled sparring sessions sharpened their skills. My students grew to appreciate the hands-on knowledge they received in a controlled setting. It was a better learning environment than throwing them in the ring against a seasoned fighter to get beat on and be exposed to injury. I never allowed it as a coach.

If you are a new student in martial arts, enjoy the journey. Don't be in a hurry to learn. You cannot be quick to learn the art. It is like learning to drive. It takes a while to become comfortable behind the wheel before you take your first driver's test. It takes longer for you to become a skilled defensive driver.

EPILOGUE

The more you practice, the better you'll be. The same applies to martial arts, except it starts over with each belt ranking you earn. As you advance in belt rankings, focus on the small details of balance, movement, and strikes. Are you consistent and focused in your training regime? Are you relaxed, fluid, and accurate, or just going through the motions? Do you understand what the movements mean in action?

The biggest obstacle for beginners is to overcome their fear. The fear of failure is powerful. It's like the first time you are called to speak in front of class at school. It can be overwhelming. But just like a classroom, the martial arts school is a controlled environment. It is the best place to learn by doing, fighting against another to test your skills. Embrace the challenge and enjoy the ride. Who knows? You might win a few sparring sessions and come to embrace the arts. Martial arts can give you an edge in life.

◆

If you are a black belt or pro fighter, ask yourself, "What have I learned about myself?" Your first real fight will tell you (and your trainer) about yourself. Are you hungry to learn more, or are you second-guessing your commitment to the fight game? Are you training regularly, or only under supervision? When you received your black belt certificate, did you hang it up on the wall or put it in a drawer? Did you think about stopping your training, or have you continued to advance? Are you teaching other belts to help them achieve their goals? If not, why not?

Many people don't know how to handle the responsibilities that having a black belt demands. In the 1960s, '70s, and '80s, martial arts training in the United States sought to weed out the weak. The schools wanted only the best students to represent them. Only the best could earn a black belt.

Today, some studios sell you a black belt based on your time spent training and passing superficial measurements of achievement. I call them *peacocks*. They are pretty birds, but not birds of prey. Unless you test yourself against others of equal experience and skill, you do not know if your martial arts abilities work. You can never know what style or form is good, because you have not challenged yourself against other fighters. How, then, can you teach others as a black belt with only prideful confidence and in-house sparring? Tournaments provide that feedback.

As masters, we should consider our path a privilege and an honor to teach. We are taking our students' lives in our hands. What you teach is not simply fighting skills. Masters teach self-discipline. We teach self-esteem and confidence. We teach physical fitness and conditioning. Above all, we teach rhythm (timing) and distance, what Bruce Lee considered the core of martial arts.

Many times in my career, parents have thanked me for the change in their child or teen's behavior; how a student was able to defuse or stop an attack from an angry patron at a restaurant or school function. Martial arts schools are more than a business. What we teach works outside the class. The longer you have a student, the more they will make the art part of their life. I remember the teachers I had in high school—the good ones and the bad. What kind of martial arts teacher are you?

True martial arts masters are comfortable with what they know. They share with other masters their techniques and forms. The best masters teach students how to learn. The best teachers want *quality* training, not just *quantity* training. Spending hours a day training without improvement is unwise. Repetition is a good thing, but refinement and change are better.

EPILOGUE

Can a black belt learn a better way to jab or counterpunch from a boxer? Can we learn, from a judo master, a better way to throw a combatant? Of course, we can. Masters should teach students to teach themselves. To keep what works, to constantly add to what they've already learned. All of us should look forward to learning something new. To humble ourselves and be open to learn new techniques to be better masters of the fighting arts.

For me, the essence of LimaLama is not just in the physical training of flowing hands and constant motion. It also is a mentality that allows LimaLama masters to remain open to change and add new fighting skills. This mindset allows students to master techniques more suited to their individual strengths and size, not locked into a specific regime. They are open to experimenting with different fighting techniques. LimaLama offers that for students, because each school throughout the Americas has its own unique program.

LimaLama has grown to have various styles in Mexico. Like Kung Do Lama, Makapi, Imua, and others in Guatemala, Honduras, Spain, and even Australia. All are effective LimaLama martial arts fighting forms. Unfortunately, some masters prefer to teach only their specific curriculum and ignore other schools. I think its wiser for all of us to share effective techniques and thereby improve each other's fighting system? From my experience, the best seminar is when all the masters share one or two effective techniques and counters. The students can practice together to understand the technique and easily add it to their personal fighting arsenal. This kind of training benefits all the schools.

What is LimaLama? Every black belt who has trained in LimaLama has a different viewpoint of what it means to them.

Some say LimaLama is 70 percent hands and 30 percent kicks. That is probably true. It is also explosive, fluid, fast, and accurate. But when I began learning other fighting arts—boxing, Ba Gua, Muay Thai, and kickboxing—I realized each new style gave me an additional skill set I could incorporate for fighting. My LimaLama improved.

LimaLama is the art of attacking, not the art of self-defense. But I couldn't sell the "Art of Attacking" to the general public. That is why I added the words *Self Defense*, as part of my school's name. It may have been deceptive advertising, but I knew few parents would want to bring their children to learn how to attack people.

When I started training students, I purposely tried to make the training of hands and kicks evenly split. The heritage of Samoan fighting included kicks that were low and effective. I learned early that kicking was an easy way to break the balance of my opponent. But the flowing hand motion of lua (Kapu Kuialua) and its intended bone-breaking techniques, were the foundation of LimaLama.

◆

Martial arts is the *art of war*, a physical means to stop an enemy. At its worst, it is a deadly means to end a threat. In reality, for most accomplished martial artists, we prepare to fight so that we won't have to fight. It is one of the ironies of my LimaLama journey. The more I learned, the less important it was for me to engage pendejos (idiots). But if someone challenged me to a fight or attacked me, then I'd oblige them, quickly. I never feared fighting or ran from a fight; I embraced it.

I have told many people that LimaLama was never an internal art. It began as an external fighting art and remains so today. LimaLama had its beginning from lua and Chinese traditions—traditions that accentuated the essence of self-control,

EPILOGUE

respect for others, and outlook to strive for the best in life. Martial arts are part of an Eastern tradition that emphasizes the fortification of the mind, body, and spirit. Similarly, LimaLama incorporates the Japanese Samurai principles of bushido, *way of the warrior*.

I have endeavored to live my life and demonstrate these principles with my students: honesty, righteousness, loyalty, honor, respect, courage, and consistency. I never sought to show off to impress anyone. On reflection, I was neither predator nor prey after earning my black belt. I found a measure of peace and gratitude, sharing my knowledge with my peers and a younger generation of fighters. I had unknowingly begun my search and practice in the internal arts, a never-ending pursuit for peace and happiness that remains true today.

Great-Grandmaster Tino once told me that LimaLama was for poor people. Poor people had a history and purpose for training to fight. It was an unconscious resolve to be protected because they lived in neighborhoods filled with violence and despair. The money spent to train and compete had value because they or their parents worked hard to earn the money to pay for training. The martial arts commitment was born of their life experience that demanded more meaning from their lives. They may have been born of humble and impoverished backgrounds, but martial arts provided them self-confidence and a positive outlook on life. This was my experience as a young man and why my legacy has been the way of martial arts, the way of a LimaLama warrior.

THE CALIFORNIA MARTIAL ARTS PIONEERS

1950s THROUGH THE 70s saw the proliferation of "hybrid" marital art styles created in California. The forerunners of these fighting evolutions we believe started with these pioneers:

Bruce Lee, Chinese name Li Jun Fan, was born November 27, 1940, in San Francisco, California. He soon became a popular American-born film actor who was renowned for his martial arts prowess and who helped promote martial arts movies in the 1970s.

Although born in San Francisco, Lee grew up in Hong Kong. He was introduced to the entertainment industry at an early age, as his father was an opera singer and part-time actor. As a teenager, he took up with local gangs and began studying Wing Chung under celebrated Grandmaster Ip Man. He also started dance lessons, which further refined his footwork and balance; in 1958, Lee won the Hong Kong Cha-Cha championship.

Lee returned to the United States shortly after he turned 18. He lived with family friends in Seattle, where he finished high school and studied philosophy and drama at the University of Washington. While in Seattle, he opened his first martial arts school, and in 1964 he relocated to Oakland, California, to found a second school. It was about that time that he developed his own technique—*Jeet Kune Do*—a blend of ancient kung fu, fencing, boxing, and philosophy. Lee began teaching his new style instead of traditional martial arts. He drew the attention of a television producer after giving a kung fu demonstration at a Los Angeles–area karate tournament, and he was cast as the sidekick Kato in the television series *The Green Hornet* (1966–67).

He returned to Hong Kong in 1971. There Lee starred in two films that broke box-office records throughout Asia, and he later found success in the United States with *Fists of Fury* (1971), *The Big Boss* and *The Chinese Connection* (1972). Lee used his sudden box-office clout to form his own production company, and in 1972 he coproduced, directed, wrote, and starred in his next film, *Return of the Dragon* (US), or *The Way of the Dragon* (Hong Kong). Lee's following film, *Enter the Dragon* (1973), was the first joint venture between Hong Kong- and US-based production companies, and it became a worldwide hit. His legacy lives on through his many books on martial arts philosophy.

John Leoning is credited with bringing *Kajukenbo* to the mainland from Hawaii in 1957. The men credited with the founding of Kajukenbo are Sijo Adriano D. Emperado, who practiced Kenpo and Escrima; Peter Young Yil Choo, who studied Korean martial arts and boxing; Joe Holck, who studied the Kodokan Judo and jiu-jitsu with Professor Okazaki; Frank Ordonez, of Kaheka Lane Danzan Ryu jiu-jitsu; and George Chang, who studied Sil Lum Pai gung fu. Kajukenbo came together in the Halawa Veterans Housing Area of Hawaii during the years 1947 through 1949. They developed one system that would complement each of their individual styles, and it had to allow for effective street fighting in the rough neighborhood of the Palama Settlement on the island of Oahu.

John Leoning developed some well-known students, such as, the actor Robert Conrad from the TV series *Hawaiian Eye*, *The Wild Wild West*, and *Black Sheep Squadron*. The first time Kajukenbo was displayed on TV was on the *Wild Wild West* TV series. One notable fight was between Conrad and the actor Robert Stroud, a Kajukenbo black belt under Sijo Emperado. Leoning's student Carlos Bunda was the first lightweight black belt champion at Ed Parker's International Karate Championships. Bunda was one of the few men to beat Chuck Norris in tournament competition. Leoning's student Mutsuto "Bill" Ryusaki is probably best known as the instructor of Benny "the Jet" Urquidez and his brothers and sister. Benny and his sister Lilly were both world kickboxing champions.

Edmund Kealoha Parker (March 19, 1931 – December 15, 1990) is considered by many as the Father of American Kenpo, with the greatest modern-day influence on the spread of Kenpo around the world. He has often been referred to as a "genius of motion," and he made meaningful contributions to the martial arts world.

He was born in Honolulu, Hawaii, on March 19, 1931. At age 16, already a black belt in judo, he had his first introduction to the art of Kenpo through Frank Chow. Parker quickly learned everything Frank could teach him, and Frank soon arranged for his more experienced brother, William Chow, to help Parker reach a higher level. The Chow brothers had been taught Kempo by Grandmaster James Mitose.

In 1919, as a young Hawaiian, Mitose was sent to Kyushu in Japan to learn his ancestors' art of Kosho Ryu Kempo. After completing his training in Japan, Mitose returned to Hawaii and in 1937 opened the "Official Self-Defense" club in Honolulu, where he called his art Kenpo Jujitsu. It was here that one of his students, William Chow, studied the art.

William "Thunderbolt" Chow was not the average martial artist. He was a street fighter who liked to test the effectiveness of his skills by making regular visits to Honolulu Chinatown to challenge the Chinese instructors as well as boisterous US military personnel. He understood that there was no "sport" in street fighting and trained accordingly. William Chow called his art Chinese Kenpo Karate.

Kenpo Karate translates as *way of the fist and empty hand*. To differentiate themselves from the traditional Japanese and Okinawan karate styles, both Mitose and Chow introduced the wearing of a black uniform (gi). This was to represent that Kenpo was more of a "war art" than the increasingly sports-oriented karate styles in white uniforms.

Parker was one of only six people to be promoted to black belt by Chow. Chow imparted in Parker the necessity for change in the Kenpo system to meet the modern needs of the American fighter. Parker made numerous contributions of innovative concepts and principles to the Kenpo system. He further refined and defined the techniques of Chinese Kenpo into a format that could be broken down into levels for all students. He called this art American Kenpo Karate.

In 1964, Ed Parker held his first International Karate Championships (IKC) in Long Beach, California, which became the largest martial arts tournament in the US for many years. The IKC brought out some of the best martial artists from around the world. Parker had met and become friends with Bruce Lee before the first IKC event.

The two had trained together and exchanged ideas on how innovation should be applied to the traditional martial arts. By Parker's invitation, Bruce Lee was given center stage at the IKC tournament and provided his first demonstration of kung fu, Wing Chung skills to the American public.

Parker is credited with establishing the American Kenpo Karate Association, which continues to thrive today around the world.

Mutsuto "Bill" Ryusaki is one of the true pioneers of Kenpo in the United States. Bill Ryusaki was born October 14, 1936, in Kamuela, on the big island of Hawaii. Bill's father, Torazo Ryusaki, held black belts in both judo and Shotokan Karate, and required all his seven sons (he also had four daughters) to train in two styles of martial arts. At the age of eight, Bill Ryusaki began training in judo and Kenpo Karate, and was taught by William Chow, Bill Chun Sr., and Marino Tiwanak.

After coming to the mainland in the late 1950s, he started training with Ed Parker in his garage. He also trained with Ed Tabian, a student of Ed Parker's. He then trained in 1957 under John Leoning (a black belt under Adriano D. Emperado), the first Kajukenbo instructor on the mainland. GM Bill Ryusaki received his black belt in Kajukenbo/Kenpo from John Leoning in 1961.

Bill has appeared in numerous films as an actor and stuntman, including television work with Bruce Lee on *The Green Hornet*; in *Hawaii 5-0* and *Wild Wild West*; with David Carradine in *Kung Fu*; and *Knots Landing*. Movie credits include *China Beach, Planet of the Apes, Above the Law, Rambo—First Blood Part II, Karate Kid II, Showdown in Little Tokyo, Robocop II, Black Rain, Double Impact, Welcome to Paradise, Universal Soldier*, and many more.

GM Ryusaki has taught his art to thousands of students, including Sensei Dan Guzman, Sensei Otto Schumann, Sensi Benny "The Jet" Urquidez, and Master Cecil Peoples. He is the founder of his own system, Ryu Dojo, Hawaiian Kenpo. GM Ryusaki holds a 10th degree (ju-dan) in Hawaiian Kenpo and, a 7th degree in judo, as well as black belts in Shotokan and aikido.

Ark Yuey Wong was born in Canton, China. GM Wong was a Registered Master (Sipak) of the Five Families or Ancestors: Choy (stances), Fut (palm arts), Li (strong, quick blocking), Hung-Gar (punching), and Mok (kicking). GM Wong also taught Sil-Lum (Five Animals)—Dragon, Snake, Tiger, Leopard, and Crane.

His home village was Toysun Tien Cum Chien. His grandfather, the head of the family, wanted all males to learn kung fu. His well-to-do family was worried by the persistent threat of bandits in the area. A family dispute had precipitated the rule that each Wong member would start kung fu training the same time they began their schooling. Young Ark Yuey took to this immediately and started training at the local Shaolin Temple. He began training with Lam Ark Fun, an elder teacher in Choy Lai Fut. Both kung fu and herbal medicine were taught by his teacher. Wong used this medical knowledge for the remainder of his life. Another teacher was Ho Ark Yeng, a leading Mok Gar instructor. Both these men had been hired to teach Wong family members.

Ark Yuey attended college at the age of 17. During this time, he taught kung fu privately and had the opportunity to meet Pang, chief monk of Canton and esteemed as one of China's top fighters. He spent a year and half with Pang. It was then that Pang demonstrated more internal powers such as action at a distance. This was Wong's first exposure to the Nei Gong art form.

Ark Yuey decided to open a local kung fu school. When his fellow teachers saw his Lion Dance demonstration (a favorite of Wong's) at a festival, he was elected a "Master," at the age of 19. In 1921, Wong arrived in the United States. He learned acupuncture and herbs from his uncle in California. He treated many people, along with teaching Lion and Dragon dancing to the Chinese community. He also taught the Five Ancestors

Boxing. Wong made a name for himself during and after World War II in the California Chinese communities of Oakland, San Francisco, and Stockton. Finally, he ended up in Los Angeles, initially teaching his fighting art only to Wong family members. In 1931, he returned to China to teach his family members. Then, in 1934, he returned to L.A. and began a long attendance at his school in Chinatown. In fact, he opened his school to *all* people interested in kung fu in the early 1960s. In doing so, he was one of the first teachers in the world to offer kung fu outside the Chinese community.

THE MASTERS

I AM HONORED AND FORTUNATE to have known many martial arts grandmasters and masters who were influential in my life as a fighter. The following list are a few of the masters, opponents, trainers, or promoters I encountered throughout my fighting career, some of whom are highlighted in this book.

THE URQUIDEZ FAMILY

Arnold Urquidez was born in 1941 and had worked for the WKA. Arnold fought at a tournament in 1968 in Chicago, losing against James Koncevic. In 1968, during a competition between Mainland and Hawaii, Arnold won two fights against Yosoke Soga and Stanley Sogai, before losing against Homer Leong. Arnold lost against Chuck Norris during a karate championship fight. He won the 1970 heavyweight title at the Internationals. He managed the team, Urquidez Bros., which took part as a team in multiple tournaments. He was a great full-contact karate fighter who traveled to China and helped train the Chinese Boxing Team.

Benny "The Jet" Urquidez is a world-renowned American kickboxer, martial arts choreographer, and actor. Benny Urquidez is creator of Ukidokan Karate. He holds black belts in judo, Kenpo under GM Ed Parker, taekwondo, LimaLama under GM Tino Tuiolosega, kung fu, jiu-jitsu, aikido, and karate. All by the age of fourteen, Benny began a storied career in the martial arts community that continues today. During his professional career from 1974 to 1993, Benny documented an incredible record in full-contact fights or kickboxing: 57 victories, 0 defeat and 0 draw, with 49 knockouts and 3 no-contests. He professes to have a record of 63–0, with 49 knockouts. The numbers don't matter; he was a bad ass in and out of the ring.

His exceptional energy and force earned him the nickname "The Jet" after one of his peers witnessed the speed and accuracy of his legendary jump-spinning back kick. By 1977, Benny had traveled the world and systematically defeated every world champion, winning the PKA and WKA titles. Urquidez, was a fearless competitor who helped pioneer full-contact fighting in the United States. He is an exceptional trainer and promoter. Benny is considered to be a scholar of martial arts fighting techniques.

Blinky Rodriguez was married to Lilly Urquidez. He had a background in karate and boxing. He fought in karate and kickboxing tournaments and finished his fighting history with a record of 34 victories with 16 knockouts and 6 defeats. He fought in super middleweight championship fights against Bill Wallace (controversial loss) and Rob Kaman (knocked out, second round), with one win by knockout against Jean-Yves Theriault. He worked me out one time and bruised my ribs trying to polish my left hook strikes. Whenever we were together, we'd always talk tactics and strategy for fights.

Lilly Urquidez was trained in Kenpo, then Shotokan and judo. She fought full contact as a super bantamweight (win against Carlotta Lee, in 1977, via TKO in the fourth round; lost against Marion Bermudez; win against Reiko Tachibana in 1977; win against Saskia Van Rijswijk in 1982; and defeat against Lucia Rijkers, by TKO in the first round, in 1983). She would have a record of 32 fights with 2 defeats. I give her credit for helping me on my footwork as a kickboxer.

Ruben Urquidez, a great fight promoter, invited me to be part of his fighting team. We co-promoted a lot of fights. The Jet Center took some smoker programs that were too large for my gym. I helped them with a large tournament, Night of the Heavyweights. It went smooth with about 15 fights. Another one was called the Beauty and the Beasts. Ruben and I became close friends. Eventually, the family wanted my El Monte gym to be part of the Jet center. My gym would have been called the *Jet Center #2*. But I couldn't afford the franchise costs.

Smiley Urquidez, the youngest of the Urquidez clan, trained in karate and kickboxing. He refereed my last kickboxing championship fight, the undercard of the Freddie La Rouch vs Benny Urquidez Championship fight.

OTHER MEMORABLE MASTERS I'VE KNOWN

Robert Alcazar, a boxing trainer, is best known for preparing Oscar de la Hoya for the Olympics, where he took the gold medal and went on to earn several world boxing titles thereafter. He was my trainer for many of my early kickboxing fights.

Abe Belardo, chief instructor, 6th Dan (SKIF), 4th Dan (Uquidokan) and, 1st Dan (Goju Ryu), was a promoter for regional martial arts and kickboxing fights in central California.

Curtis Faust was originally from Arkansas. He received a black belt under GM Sal Esquivel, and he trained with Ron Van Cliff, the "Black Dragon."

Steve Fisher is a 7th degree black belt in Shōrin-Ryū Karate. He trained under International Champions Tadashi Yamashita and Mike Stone.

Refugio Flores was a 5th degree black belt in Kenpo Karate under Ed Parker. He became a world champion in kickboxing. He was a successful fight trainer and promoter.

Dan Guzman, a Kajukenbo/Kempo Grandmaster, studied under GM Ray Ryusaki and Joe Rosas. He is grandmaster to many well-known Kajukenbo black belts, including LimaLama Masters Richard Nuñez and Sal Esquivel.

Sonny Hughes is a 10th degree Hanshi in jiu-jitsu and judo.

Mimi Lesseos, an American female professional wrestler, actress, model, and stuntwoman, was also an International Full Contact Martial Arts champion. I consulted with her during two of her fight scenes for movies.

Danny "Magic" Lopez trained under Don Wilson in gung fu. He boxed professionally for a short time and captured two kickboxing world title belts as a welterweight. Danny worked for many years as a stuntman in Hollywood. Today, he is a producer, director, stunt coordinator, and editor. He continues to train MMA fighters on their hand and leg work.

Eddie Mápula, a grandmaster, is a 10th degree black belt and a three-time World Kickboxing/Karate champion. He has over 42 years in the martial arts, of which 27 years were spent working in the Chuck Norris organization. He has been inducted into the USA Martial Arts, Taekwondo, KRO1 and Tijuana–Baja-California Halls of Fame. Eddie is the founder and president of Black Belt Development and is a life coach instructor.

Tom Ramirez received his black belt from me. He was also the best man in my wedding. He earned his 3rd degree under my tutelage and was later promoted under GM Esquivel and later with GM Nuñez. He eventually earned his 6th degree under GGM Tuiolosega.

THE MASTERS

Miguel Reyes earned his black belt under GGM Rigoberto Lopez. Reyes was a Tijuana Hall of Fame trainer and promoter, and he earned a world title in the Super Lightweight division.

Danny Rodarte earned a 5th degree black belt under GM Ed Parker in Kenpo Karate. He created the International Kickboxing Association (IKBA) and was its vice-president. In 1974, Rodarte opened his first Kenpo Karate Studio. He was also a co-founder of the Tournament Promoters Association (TPA) in southern California. Rodarte is best known as a promoter and one of the key founders of kickboxing in the United States.

Greg Spence earned his black belt under GGM Tino Tuiolosega. He accepted the Black Belt Hall of Fame award in Las Vegas on behalf of GGM Tuiolosega after he passed away. Master Spence was an aggressive competitor in point-system competitions.

Scott Thorson, with no formal training in martial arts or boxing, turned to kickboxing as a means to relieve pent-up anger and frustration in his life. I was his trainer when he became a kickboxing champion as a Super Lightweight, Lightweight, and Welterweight during the 1990s.

Frank Trejo earned his black belt in Kenpo Karate under GM Ed Parker. He was a trainer in many fights for Promoter Danny Rodarte.

Hector Ventoura studied Chinese Kenpo in 1972 under Alfredo Duarte in El Salvador for 13 years. Sensei Duarte studied under Carlos Navarro from Hawaii, whose mentor, Rafael Castro, studied under William Chow and James Mitose. Sensei Ventoura came to the United States in early 1982. Master Ted Tabura met Hector at a martial arts tournament, and both realized they were neighbors in Glendale. Sensei Ventoura was refereeing some of the competitions at the time. Tabura became friends with Hector and introduced Sensei to GM Tino Tuiolosega. Tabura took Sensei Hector to a LimaLama tournament in Riverside, where he first observed the martial art. He was introduced to me in 1982–83 at a tournament at the Jet Center. It was at the Jet Center that Hector also first met Sensei Tadashi Yamashita. Sensei Hector combined his LimaLama training with Chinese Kenpo and created his own fighting art called *Ming Shuang Tao*. We remain close friends to this day.

Jimmy H. Woo was the Grandmaster of San Soo Kung Fu. (See *Glossary of Terms*-San Soo)

Tadashi Yamashita currently retains the rank of 10th degree black belt in Okinawa Shōrin-Ryū Karatedo and 10th degree black belt in Zen Okinawa Kobudo. Sensei Yamashita is the past president and director of US Shorin-Ryu Karate Association, the USA President of the Zen Okinawan Kobudo Association, and former Chief Instructor of Shōrin-Ryūin the United States. Sensei Yamashita combined many progressive fighting tactics (one of which was LimaLama) with traditional aspects of karatedo, thus resulting in a devastating fighting system. Sensei's dynamic fighting system known as Suikendo, which translates to *fist flowing like water*, is a non-stop flowing system of fighting. It allows the trained fighter to simultaneously block and strike his opponent with blinding speed and accuracy.

ACKNOWLEDGMENTS

WE ARE FOREVER GRATEFUL for the support and advice from the following martial arts masters that helped make this book possible: Al Garza, 8th degree grandmaster in LimaLama for the historical overview on the life of Tino Tuiolosega; GM Garza documented the early years of LimaLama and shared an intimate chronology of GGM Tino's martial arts journey. Ming Shuang Tao, Sensi Hector Ventoura shared his array of photographic and personal stories about GGM Tino and his students. Likewise, we are forever grateful to GM Rigoberto Lopez, the Father of LimaLama in Mexico, for his first-hand discussion on the systemizing of LimaLama training.

Thanks to our beta readers, Irene Fosdick, Gabriel Gutierrez, Juanita Ynigues, Lucy Herrera, and Mary Ellen "Nena" Lawler, for pointing out the obvious and not so obvious flaws in our chapters. A heartfelt thanks to our copy editor, Lynette Smith, for her professional clean-up of our writing. Finally, a special thanks to our publishing consultant, David Wogahn of Author Imprints, whose able team ironed out the details for the book production and release.

Special thanks to Sensei Mike Matsuda for his timely critique of our book cover concept; and likewise to Yvette Dominguez for her creative work in making a one-of-a-kind book cover design. Finally, much gratitude to all the martial artists who were interviewed about their chosen disciplines and were willing to share with the world the external and internal beauty and strength of martial arts and their sincere reflections about Lorenzo "Coach" Rodriguez.

We missed many first-hand remembrances with the passing of Richard Nuñez in 2022 and Kiypo Tuiolosega in 2023, during the production of this book. Likewise, notable fighters and masters may not be listed among the many who trained under GGM Tino and GM Rigo. Any omissions, mistakes, and/or opinions belong to us. If we failed in our historical accounts, we did so unknowingly. Rather, it has been our hope to elevate awareness about the many fighters and teachers who have come from the martial art world, especially the relatively unknown but emerging martial art, LimaLama.

Lorenzo "Coach" Rodriguez
Grandmaster, LimaLama

Richard A. Alvarado
Editor-In-Chief,
Órale Press

GLOSSARY OF TERMS

Amateur Athletic Union (AAU)—an alliance of national and district associations, amateur athletic groups, and educational institutions formed in the United States in 1888 for the purpose of certifying athletes as amateurs in various sports.

Ba Gua Quan (*also known as* Ba Gua, Baguazhang, and Pa Kua Chuan)—one of the three main Chinese martial arts of the Wudang school, the other two being t'ai chi and xing yi quan. It is more broadly grouped as an internal practice. Bāguà zh□ng literally means *eight trigram palm*, referring to the trigrams of the *I Ching*, one of the canons of Taoism. The creation of Baguazhang as a formalized martial art is attributed to Dong Haichuan, who is said to have learned from Taoist and Buddhist masters in the mountains of rural China during the early 19th century. Although the many branches of Baguazhang are often quite different from each other (some, like Cheng style, specialize in close-in wrestling and joint locks; while others, like some of the Yin styles, specialize in quick, long-range striking), all have circle walking, spiraling movement, and certain methods and techniques (piercing palms, crashing palms, etc.) in common.

Baguazhang contains an extremely wide variety of techniques as well as weapons, including various strikes (with palm, fist, elbow, fingers, etc.), kicks, joint locks, throws, and distinctively evasive circular footwork. As such, Baguazhang is considered neither a purely striking nor a purely grappling martial art. Baguazhang practitioners are known for their ability to "flow" in and out of the way of objects. This is the source of the theory of being able to fight multiple attackers. Baguazhang's evasive nature is also shown by the practice of moving behind an attacker, so that the opponent cannot harm the practitioner.

Grandmaster (GM)—a high ranking (usually black belt degrees of seven or higher) in martial arts.

Great-Grandmaster (GGM)—This designation is reserved for the founders of a martial art style. Usually having three or more generations of black belts under their system.

International Kickboxing Association (IKBA)—created by promoter Danny Rodarte. He received his 1st degree black belt in Kenpo Karate from Ed Parker in 1969. In 1974, Rodarte opened his first Kenpo Karate Studio. Rodarte was also a cofounder of the Tournament Promoters Association (TPA) in southern California. Rodarte was one of the pioneers of US full-contact kickboxing events in southern California, including the very first Western US–Thai kickboxing event in Hawaii. Rodarte organized and promoted the first officially licensed Thai kickboxing event at the Los Angeles Olympic Auditorium.

International Kickboxing Federation (IKF)—founded in 1992 by Steve Fossum and Dan Stell in Northern California. Stell eventually stepped down to go back to fighting, while Fossum continued with the organization. In 1999, Fossum and Joe Taylor of Ringside Products created the first amateur open

GLOSSARY OF TERMS

North American tournament for Kickboxing and Muay Thai, now the IKF World Classic.

Karate—An Asian system of unarmed combat using hand and feet to deliver blows. It was formalized in Okinawa in the 17th century. It was imported into Japan in the 1920s. Several schools and karate systems developed, each favoring somewhat different techniques and training methods.

Katas—a structured form of dance designed to showcase martial arts techniques.

Kajukenbo—a hybrid martial art from Hawaii. It was developed in the late 1940s and founded in 1947 in the Palama Settlement of Palama, Hawaii. The name Kajukenbo is a combination of the various arts from which its style is derived: *ka* for karate, *ju* for judo and jiu-jitsu, *ken* for Kenpo, and *bo* for boxing.

Kenpo (*also known as* **Kempo**)—a unique hybrid of Japanese and Chinese karate. In America, Ed Parker created American Kenpo Karate. Also known as American Kenpo or Kenpo Karate. It is an updated system of martial arts based on modern-day street fighting that applies logic and practicality. It is characterized by the use of quick and powerful strikes delivered from all of the body's natural weapons, powered by rapid stance transitions. Parker made significant modifications to the original art of Kenpo throughout his life, by introducing or changing principles, theories, and concepts of motion, as well as terminology. Parker left behind a large following of instructors who honored his teachings by implementing many different versions of American Kenpo.

Kenpo Si Lama—created by GGM Tuiolosega in the 1990s. It incorporates aspects of lua, Kajukenbo, and Sil Lum with LimaLama techniques.

Kickboxing—American kickboxing originated in the 1970s and was brought to prominence in September 1974 when the Professional Karate Association (PKA) held the first World Championships. Historically, kickboxing can be considered a hybrid martial art formed from the combination of elements of traditional styles of boxing, martial arts, and Muay Thai. Kickboxing became increasingly popular among active martial arts fighters during the 1970s. It allowed for full contact in tournaments without judges determining points for near strikes. Kickboxing was the precursor of mixed martial arts (MMA) that led to further hybridization incorporating ground fighting techniques from judo, jiu-jitsu, and wrestling.

Kobudo—literally meaning "ancient martial way," kobudo refers to the weapons art of the Okinawan people. During the time when kobudo was first developed, the Japanese Satsuma Samurai had occupied Okinawa and established a ban on weapons and all martial arts practice.

Kumite—meaning "to spar," Kumite is a stylized free-form of fighting using light blows for judges to score points.

Kung fu (*also known as* **gung fu**)—a Cantonese phrase meaning, depending on context and the connotations an interpreter applies to the term, "hard work," or "human skill"; especially in the context of the martial arts, *gong* carries the meaning of "inner power." In contemporary Western usage, kung fu has been used as a generic term for Chinese martial arts ranging from what have been labeled the "soft" or "internal" arts of taijiquan (tai chi ch'uan), baguazhang (pa kua ch'uan), and xingyiquan (hsing i ch'uan) to the so-called hard or external arts of Northern and Southern Shaolin. The term *kung fu* has been associated particularly with those martial systems that tradition claims are descended from the Shaolin Temple arts. In addition, the label *kung fu* tends to be more strongly associated, outside China at least, with the forms of Chinese martial arts that are presumed to emphasize striking over grappling techniques.

Master (M)—A high ranking black belt in martial arts.

Professional Karate Association (PKA; *later called* **Professional Karate and Kickboxing Association)**—created in 1974 by Joe Corley, Dan Quin, and Judy Quin. The organization promoted professional karate and kickboxing events. Notable early participants included Jeff Smith, Bill Wallace, Joe Lewis, Jerry Piddington, Benny "The Jet" Urquidez, The Ice Man, Jean-Yves Thériault, Dennis "the Terminator" Alexio, and many more.

Professional Karate League (PKL)—created by Chuck Norris. Only Black Belts were allowed to compete. The first show was held in Hawaii, and the LA Stars was the first group from California.

San Soo (*also known as* **Sanshou**)—Kung Fu San Soo was created by Chin Siu Dek, who took the name Jimmy Haw Woo upon entering the United States in the early 1900s. San Soo is a distinct Chinese-American fighting style that is based on techniques from Northern and Southern Chinese martial arts systems. It is a concentrated version of Tsoi Li Ho Fut Hung and Hung Sing Goon styles of kung fu.

Sifu/Sensei—a master or grandmaster of high ranking in martial artists from Korea, China, or Japan.

Shōrin-Ryū Karate—one of the major modern Okinawa martial arts and oldest styles of karate. It was named by Chosin Chibana in 1933 but is considered to be much older. Notable descendants are Shotokan and American Kenpo.

Suikendo (*pronounced* **See-kan-doe**)—Sensei Tadashi Yamashita's personally developed style of martial arts. Suikendo combines elements of combat, balance, and agility; it develops strength, flexibility, and a combat-alert spirit. The word *suikendo* means "the way of the fist that flows like water." This word, and its meaning, encompasses the philosophy and the concept of this style; the body remains centered while the hands and feet practice multiple striking and breaking techniques in a fluid and fast manner, imitating the sense of water falling from high above. The essence of the techniques used in Suikendo are an enhanced extract of a sophisticated study of Shōrin-Ryū.

World Kickboxing Association (WKA)—Howard Hansen created the WKA. He stepped down in 1992.

REFERENCES

"Ark Yuey Wong: 01/11/1900 to 01/11/1987" (N.A.). Retrieved June 5, 2023, from https://www.plumpub.com/kaimen/ark-yuey-wong/.

Buck, Phil. "Fighting Arts of the Pacific Islands." Retrieved June 5, 2023, from http://www.wama-club.com/pacificfightingartsarticle.htm.

Buck, Phil (with thanks to Lee Wedlake). "Kenpo and Jeet Kune Do: A Comparison." Retrieved June 5, 2023, from https://kenpotv.com/kenpo-and-jeet-kune-do-a-comparison/.

"Ed Parker Sr: Teacher, Author, and Promoter" (N.A.). Retrieved June 5, 2023, from https://www.usadojo.com/ed-parker-sr/.

Garza, Al (Producer). *Lima Lama 1974 Classic: By Founder/Grandmaster Tino Tuiolosega*. Video.

Garza, Al. *My Story: Memories of a Martial Art Grandmaster*. Pikesville, MD: Sefer Press, 2015.

"Historical Limalama Notes and Photos." (N.A.). Retrieved June 5, 2023, from https://web.archive.org/web/20090529061739/http://www.wama-club.com/limalama_history.htm.

Kenpo Dragon. Retrieved June 5, 2023, from https://www.kenpo.com.au/.

Leonard, George. *Mastery: The Keys to Success and Long-Term Fulfillment.* New York, NY: Plume, 1992.

Ley, Rodney. "Beware the Whipping Hands of Lima Lama." *Black Belt,* May 1999, pp. 82–87–95–169.

Little, John (Ed.). *Bruce Lee: Letters of The Dragon, An Anthology of Bruce Lee's Correspondence with Family, Friends, and Fans, 1958–1973.* Rutland, VT: Tuttle Publishing, 2016.

Little, John (Ed.). *Bruce Lee: Words of The Dragon, Interviews and Conversations 1958–1973.* Rutland, VT: Tuttle Publishing. 2017.

"Pa Kua Chuan, 8 Trigram Form, Introduction" (N.A.). Retrieved June 5, 2023, from https://www.chinahand.com/pakua/pakua.htm.

Polynesian Martial Arts: Ancient Tongan Boxing and Modern Samoan Wrestling, Techniques and Origins. Video retrieved 2020 from https://www.youtube.com/watch?v=kqu4friQeow.

Rubenstein, Steven. "East Side Story, Gang-Busting in the Ghetto." *Karate Illustrated,* August 1974, pp. 8–13.

"Tadashi Yamashita Sensei" (N.A.). Retrieved June 5, 2023, from http://www.tadashiyamashita.com/sensei.html.

"Tino's History: Grand Master Tu'umamao 'Tino' Tuiolosega" (N.A.). Retrieved June 5, 2023, from http://www.limalama.org/tino.html.

Totton, Carl. "LimaLama: The Modern Polynesian American Martial Art with Ancient Chinese Roots." *Inside Kung Fu Magazine,* May 2004.

"Yamashita Suikendo" (N.A.). Retrieved June 5, 2023, from https://www.yamashitamartialarts.com/suikendo.

Young, Robert. "Life and Times of American Kenpo Master Ed Parker." Retrieved June 5, 2023, from https://blackbeltmag.com/ed-parker-american-kenpo-master.

www.ingramcontent.com/pod-product-compliance
Lightning Source LLC
Chambersburg PA
CBHW072151070526
44585CB00015B/1094